the Summitt Season

the Summitt Season

Nancy E. Lay
The University of Tennessee, Knoxville

Leisure Press
Champaign, Illinois

Developmental Editor: Sue Ingels Mauck
Copy Editor: Claire M. Mount
Assistant Editor: Robert King
Production Director: Ernie Noa
Typesetter: Brad Colson
Text Design: Keith Blomberg
Text Layout: Michelle Baum
Cover Design: Jack Davis
Cover and Interior Photos: Nick Myers
Printed By: Braun-Brumfield, Inc.

ISBN: 0-88011-339-1

Library of Congress Cataloging-in-Publication Data

Lay, Nancy E., 1933-
  The Summitt season / Nancy E. Lay.
    p.   cm.
  ISBN 0-88011-339-1
  1. Summitt, Pat Head, 1952-   . 2. Basketball—United States—
Coaches—Biography. 3. Lady Volunteers (Basketball team)
I. Title.
GV884.S86L39 1989
796.32'3'0922—dc19
[B]   88-22098
                                                                          CIP

Printed in the United States of America

10 9 8 7 6 5 4 3 2 1

Leisure Press
A Division of Human Kinetics Publishers, Inc.
Box 5076, Champaign, IL 61820
1-800-342-5457
1-800-334-3665 (in Illinois)

For
Helen B. Watson
and
my family, and especially for the memory of Big Sarah
and the promise of her namesake,
Sarah Carolyn McCorkle

Contents

Acknowledgments

The three people primarily responsible for my writing this book are my high school and college basketball coaches: the late Karl Reedy of Coeburn High School, Coeburn, Virginia; and the late Fanny G. Crenshaw and the very much alive Mary Jane Miller, both of Westhampton College, University of Richmond, Virginia. All three were master teachers and coaches (my high school team won 59 straight games, and my college team had two undefeated seasons), but more important, I learned from them that a life in physical education and sport can be challenging, rewarding, fulfilling, and, above all, fun. I am very grateful to them for being, in different ways, wonderful role models.

Individuals at the University of Tennessee, Knoxville, who deserve special recognition for their contributions to the project are Buck Jones and Joan Paul, former and present heads of the department of physical education and dance, who were very supportive; Joe Rader, head of circulation services, Hodges Library, for assigning me a faculty study in the magnificent new library, which afforded a quiet place to write; Felicia Felder-Hoene, reference librarian, for patiently searching out answers to my many questions; Glenda Dills, secretary in the department of physical education and dance, for her computer literacy and for typing the manuscript without complaint; and my students, who shared enthusiastic interest and encouragement throughout the process of developing this book.

Colleagues at other schools who were quite helpful were Bettye Giles and Nadine Gearin at the University of Tennessee, Martin, and Jane Hooker at Memphis State University. Thanks to them for their support.

I also extend appreciation to the people who consented to be interviewed for the book for sharing their sport experiences.

My thanks go to Debby Jennings, sports information director for women's athletics at UTK. She went beyond the call of duty on many occasions, and willingly provided most of the photographs that appear in the book.

Special recognition goes to Mariah Burton Nelson, freelance writer and editor, for her revisions and integration of the manuscript, and to Sue Mauck, developmental editor at Human Kinetics, for her many contributions.

Finally, to women athletes at UTK present and past, my sincere thanks. I will always remember the 1987-88 Lady Vol basketball team with real affection. All of you—athletes, coaches, and support staff—are a great bunch. Thanks for letting me share another Summitt season.

Preface

This book was written for several reasons. Foremost is the fact that it is, to my knowledge, the first of its kind about a woman coach and a women's basketball program at a large university.

A second reason is Pat Head Summitt herself. She has had enormous success as an athlete and coach, is a fascinating personality with an interesting heritage, and has many Lady Vol fans who would like to read about her. Were Pat Summitt a man in a similar position, there would probably have been by this time in her career several biographies about her. The fact that she is relatively unknown outside of women's basketball circles says something about the struggle for women's equality in general and for women's sport in particular.

Which brings me to the third reason for the book: women's equality and acceptance in sport. Pat Summitt's career has spanned a time of tremendous growth, challenge, and change for the female athlete, but there is still much to be done before women are accepted not only by themselves but by mainstream America as being serious about this business of sport. Perhaps this book will help dispel some of those ambiguities.

My own background as an athlete, coach, and athletic administrator was another reason to write this book. I was the first women's athletic director at the University of Tennessee, Knoxville, and although the title of the position during my tenure (1972-76) was Coordinator of Intercollegiate Athletics, I have the distinction of having recommended that Pat Head be hired in 1974; we have been friends since that time. She has been most enthusiastic about the book and allowed me complete access to the team. She read sections of the manuscript as it was completed and corrected factual errors, but there was never any censorship. The experience has been a good one for both of us. .

Nancy E. Lay
Knoxville, Tennessee

1987 NCAA Champions: The defense begins.

CHAPTER ONE

The Defense Begins: October 15, 1987

The date specified by the National Collegiate Athletic Association for the first basketball practice at Division I schools was October 15, 1987. The University of Tennessee Lady Volunteers assembled at 6:50 a.m., in the women's dressing room.

Entering the Stokely Athletics Center dressing room, one would be struck by its smallness—if all 12 players sat on the floor to stretch, their legs would have to interlock like puzzle pieces. Each player had a designated dressing area, consisting of a small bulletin board and a peg for hanging clothes.

Over the coaches' chalkboard, on the wall between the two rows of dressing areas, was a sign: "INTENSITY." Scattered about in other strategic locations—over the mirror, over the sinks, on the door—were motivational messages: "DID I DO MY PERSONAL BEST?"; "BE ALL YOU CAN BE"; "LADY VOLS HAVE PRIDE"; "LOVE THE PRESSURE";

1

and "OFFENSE SELLS TICKETS—DEFENSE WINS GAMES." There was only one sign with any levity, written in a different hand. It said, "Are we having fun yet?"

Each dressing area was adorned with the name and the photograph of an athlete. The names, inscribed in large black letters, were a source of pride for the women, offering a sense of permanence and belonging.

It was surprising, then, that the two freshmen, Kris Durham and Pearl Moore, had not yet been assigned spaces. Instead, the names of Karla Horton, Shelley Sexton, Sabrina Mott, and Cheryl Littlejohn, last year's departing players, still hung boldly above four empty dressing areas. Neither Durham nor Moore complained, but they seemed uncomfortable about this oversight, and sat stiffly on the benches while the other players examined their designated territories.

As was true with most Lady Vol freshmen, Pearl and Kris had been high school superstars. Pearl, a 6-2 forward from nearby Harriman, Tennessee, had established Harriman High records in scoring, rebounding, blocked shots, and assists. After her astounding 4-year career, the school retired her jersey.

Number 23 Kris Durham vs. Wake Forest

Kris, who traveled south to Knoxville from Dunellen, New Jersey, broke Union Catholic Regional High School's scoring record early, in her junior year, and went on to graduate with 2,547 career points. Considered the third-best recruit in the nation, Kris arrived at Tennessee having already played on the Olympic Festival team for 2 years, and having traveled to Canada with the Junior National team, which included her new teammates Tonya Edwards, Sheila Frost, and Bridgette Gordon.

But the similarities between the two rookies ended with their high school superstar status. Pearl was a tall black forward; Kris a compact white guard. Pearl was a shy, soft-spoken southerner who despite her height was uncertain how or even if she could contribute to the Tennessee team; Kris was a confident, even cocky, easterner who had no doubt that soon, perhaps even this season, she could command the starting position at point guard. Pearl had chosen Tennessee because it was close to her family; Kris picked it because it was the best basketball school in the nation, and she planned to bring her family with her. So sure was Kris of her ability that her parents had already bought a condominium in Knoxville so they could come down from New Jersey to watch their youngest daughter play ball.

But the condo was for later, 2 months from now, when games would start. For now, Kris's task was to listen, to practice like she'd never practiced before, and to wait.

At 5-foot-10, Pat Head Summitt can be an imposing figure, even to the taller centers. She is thin—some friends say too thin—about 140 pounds, down from 165 when she was playing basketball. She dresses impeccably, even wearing the latest in warm-up suits to practice. At 35, her skin still has the smoothness of a cover girl, her steel-blue eyes are intense and impenetrable, and the set of her square jaw expresses her determination.

Her approach to this organizational meeting was all business. The two rookies had already spent considerable time with Summitt during the recruiting process and the rest of the players knew her well, so no introductions were needed; nor did Summitt feel a need to greet the players or welcome them to the season. She began the morning session by distributing handouts describing the regular 1-2-2 pattern and the two options from this pattern. Summitt discussed the offense briefly, stressing that its success depended upon spreading out to use the entire front court and making accurate adjustments to the defense. She also stressed court awareness—

knowing where all nine other players are—and the importance of players without the ball "entertaining" the defense.

While Summitt spoke, the players, seated on the benches and the floor, took notes. Summitt's assistant coaches, Holly Warlick and Mickie DeMoss, would contribute suggestions about particular strategies, as would graduate assistant Heidi Van Derveer and undergraduate assistant Shelley Sexton. Often Summitt asked questions of specific players, and, eager to please, the players were responsive.

"Dawn, what's the key to breaking a zone defense?"

"Quick passing."

"Sheila, what do you do after setting a pick?"

"Roll toward the basket, asking for the ball."

Kris Durham and Pearl Moore were equally energetic, apparently not intimidated by the situation.

The coach did not dwell on the defensive strategy but said that, because of their quickness, she expected this team to be the best defensive team she had ever coached. Last year, she said, the team's defensive play was responsible for the NCAA crown.

Because the team had been in conditioning sessions since their arrival on campus in mid-September, they had already established some camaraderie with the two new players. This first meeting, however, was restrained and serious. As champions, the team members were presented with the difficult task of defending that title, and that responsibility seemed to render joking out of the question.

The team was also subdued because 6-3 sophomore Carla McGhee, who had played an important part in the success of the 1987 team, had been injured the previous Sunday in an automobile accident. Her jaw had been broken in five places, and her cheekbone was fractured. Her playing status was dubious. The potential loss of long, lean Carla McGhee (nick-named "Leggs") was an added blow since Karla Horton, the 6-2 center on the championship team, had married and decided to forego her senior year of eligibility.

Summitt voiced concern over the loss of these two rebounders. Re-bounding by the perimeter players was a distinct weakness in last year's squad, she said, and she challenged junior forwards Bridgette Gordon and Jennifer Tuggle to improve that aspect of their game.

After Summitt's remarks, assistant coach Holly Warlick reminded the athletes that showers were mandatory after practices and games. Practice clothes were to be left in the dressing room and would be washed after each practice. She also asked players to leave towels in the locker room and not to take them to the dorms.

Number 42 Pearl Moore vs. Alabama

At precisely 7:30 a.m., the players were dismissed. Several gathered books for 7:50 classes; others returned to their dorms or other engagements. By 12:15 they would return to the gym, dressed, stretched, ankle-taped, and ready for their first practice of the season.

Tennessee's team is legendary. Not only did they win the 1987 NCAA championship, but their coach, Pat Head Summitt, is perhaps the most successful and certainly the most renowned coach in the game. She has two Olympic medals to her credit; a silver as a player in 1976, and a gold as a coach in 1984. Her Tennessee teams have reached the Final Four in 8 of the past 11 years, and her program has produced 6 Olympians, 11 all-Americans, and 21 international performers. Her overall coaching record, including international games, was 382 wins and 106 losses.

Thus even the first practice of the season drew a small crowd. As the players stretched, the 16-member girls' basketball team from Powell High School in Knoxville filed in, as did Maryville College's first-year coach, Wes Moore, and assorted women and men of unknown origins and motives. Crews from three local television stations paced the sidelines, experimenting with camera angles.

"I have no basketball secrets," Summitt repeatedly tells prospective observers. "Everybody is welcome to watch our team practice."

Converse was supplying each player with shoes and five practice shirts. Shoes were being restricted this year to three pairs per player; last year, the supply was unlimited, and Dawn Marsh and Bridgette Gordon literally ran through eight pairs apiece. Each shirt was a different color and had a different slogan on the front. Today's shirt was navy blue and read "NCAA Champs—Lady Vols 1987—Defend It." On the back was the word "Converse."

Practice would last from 12:15 to 3:15; the men's team would practice in the same facility from 3:30 to 6:30. The men had first choice of practice times, as was the case in other universities in the Southeastern Conference. Some of the women's teams practiced early in the morning or in the evening. Arch-rival Georgia, for example, practiced at night, but they did not stick to that schedule on October 15.

In her succinct greeting to her players, Pat told them that Georgia had practiced on the court at 6:00 this morning. "Aren't you glad you came to Tennessee?" A few of the athletes laughed. "We didn't begin until 6:50," she reminded them, "and then only a skull session." As an afterthought, she added, "The opposition is starting early trying to catch us. Let's get moving."

The first drill was familiar to players and fans alike since it was already used as a pregame warm-up. The purpose of this four-corner passing drill, which Summitt learned from Indiana's infamous Bobby Knight, was to develop the players' ability to pass quickly and accurately and to build excitement. As with most athletic feats performed by skilled people, this one looked deceptively easy. The pattern was complex, and it took practice and concentration to run the drill effectively. Kris and Pearl had difficulty in the beginning, pausing to think between passes or passing to the wrong corner, but they soon caught on. All three coaches were actively involved, especially Summitt, who yelled encouragement and stopped to make corrections when necessary. This set the tone for the rest of the practice.

Coach Summitt has a unique system for criticizing and praising her team during practice. Whenever criticism is given, the athlete to whom it is directed is not permitted to question Summitt or defend herself. Instead, she is expected to acknowledge the criticism with the single word "Rebound." When a player is praised, her response must be "Two points." Summitt maintains that a player never leaves the gym with more "rebounds" than "two points."

After the passing drill, the players were divided into three lines to practice full-court options off the weave, or figure-eight, pattern. Next the squad was divided into four groups: point guards, perimeter forwards, low posts, and high posts. Each group reported to one of four stations, then rotated to a new station after 4 minutes. Holly Warlick supervised the passing station; Summitt worked with the players on rebounding and tapping the ball in. Student assistant Shelley Sexton and graduate assistant Heidi Van Derveer taught footwork and agility, and assistant coach Mickie DeMoss instructed the players in the art of dribbling. At some stations, there were teaching aids: jump ropes for footwork; an eleven-pound medicine ball for passing; and for dribbling drills, plastic glasses that prevented players from seeing the ball.

The last drill before the break was a three-player transition drill. In 2 minutes the team was expected to make 40 baskets. They made 44.

During the break, players staggered to the fountains for water. Despite preseason conditioning, the first practice always comes as a bit of a shock as players exert extra energy to impress the coach. Perhaps to this end, Kris Durham ignored the water fountains and hovered under the basket, shooting.

While the coaches regrouped to discuss the progress of the practice, an athletic department secretary approached them and reported that Carla McGhee's mother had just called. Carla was in great distress, she said, because her doctor discovered a hip injury. Her face and jaw injuries had been depressing enough, but the hip injury devastated McGhee, because it would probably require traction and could destroy her basketball career. Coach Summitt immediately dispatched Holly Warlick to the hospital to talk with the injured Lady Volunteer. Warlick had helped DeMoss recruit McGhee, and Summitt believes in the importance of those recruiting relationships.

When practice resumed, Summitt introduced the most physically demanding drill. It was a 4-on-2 continuous fast break, referred to as the bungle drill, and it had become a Tennessee tradition to run it with particular gusto. The players switched quickly from offense to defense as the coach yelled "Change." After 10 minutes of almost continuous running, Pat gave the players a break for another drink. Kris Durham again chose to shoot baskets. This time Dawn Marsh joined her. Apparently the senior point guard was not to be outdone by the new recruit.

After the break, Summitt explained the 1-2-2 offensive pattern. Since the only players not familiar with the Tennessee offense were Kris and Pearl, most of the time was spent working with them. Pearl had problems with positioning, but the coaches and her teammates were sensitive to her rookie status and not demanding. Nonetheless, Pearl was nervous, and had difficulty catching the ball and making easy baskets. Kris, on the other hand, exuded confidence. She dribbled behind her back, fired crisp passes, and sank long shots. Judging from her performance, the New Jersey high school all-American could as easily have been a senior as a freshman. But she had not developed the leadership skills of an older player, and her success was met with silence from her teammates. Would Durham steal the starting position from Dawn Marsh, the popular team clown? Could the team rally behind a flashy freshman point guard? Nobody criticized Durham's hotdogging, but neither did they applaud.

Practice continued with a half-court scrimmage lasting 15 minutes. This was followed by a 3-minute full-court scrimmage. All Lady Vol practices would follow this pattern: the breakdown of offensive and defensive sets followed by the players' executing those sets in a game situation. These particular scrimmages were spirited, with lots of high-fives after good plays. Coach Summitt frequently stopped the play, however, to make suggestions.

Next Summitt demonstrated the new defensive stance. Instead of the usual parallel position of the feet, Summitt instructed the players to stagger the feet, one forward and one back, with the weight on the balls of the feet. Short, choppy steps, Summitt informed her players, are quicker than the sliding steps they had used in previous years. She pointed out that 6-foot Bridgette Gordon had the best defensive coverage in postseason play last year not because she was the quickest Tennessee player, but because her low stance enabled her to move faster than her teammates.

Gordon's teammates did not need to be reminded of her ability. The political science major from DeLand, Florida, was tenacious on defense, had led her team in scoring in her freshman and sophomore years, and was often the one to step forward for the Most Valuable Player award after a tournament. Every preseason publication had included her as a first-team all-American. Gordon simply nodded to acknowledge the coach's compliment and uttered the requisite, "Two points."

Summitt also modified the arm position of the defensive stance. In the past, Lady Vol teams kept their hands low, but now the arms were to be bent, with hands up at about head level. After demonstrating the technique, Summitt instructed the players to line up in four rows. As they shuffled awkwardly across the floor in the new stagger-footed pattern, hands in the air, Dawn Marsh shouted, "Are we moving fast yet?" It was the only funny remark during the entire practice. Coach Summitt did not acknowledge the question.

At 3:15 Coach Summitt called the squad together and reminded them that until the opening game on November 27, the Lady Vols would practice six times per week. She also explained that they would be tested for drug use periodically throughout the season, and she gave them an assignment. Before reporting for practice tomorrow, each player was to have a 15-minute mental practice session on the offensive and defensive strategies covered in today's session. Everyone huddled in the circle, placed one hand in the middle, and, after the stack of hands bounced three times, shouted, "Together!" The players then hurriedly left the gym.

As the men's team began their warm-up drill, Summitt conferred with her three assistants; the fourth, Holly Warlick, had not yet returned from the hospital. Summitt was pleased with the first practice, she said; indeed, she was ecstatic about the progress of junior forward Jennifer Tuggle. Voted "Sixth Player of the Year" by her teammates her first year at Tennessee, the 6-2 forward had torn her anterior cruciate ligament five games into her sophomore season and sat out the rest of that year. Because of an NCAA "medical hardship" rule, she was allowed to repeat her sophomore season the following year, but had a slow, lumbering stride, in part because of the knee brace. Summitt noted that in the first practice of the year Tuggle appeared to be much stronger and was playing with greater intensity and aggressiveness. Though Tuggle would never reach the distinction of her idol, Larry Bird, the sharp-shooting forward from Etowah, Tennessee, was finally playing basketball the way Summitt liked to see it. The three coaches left Stokely Gym in high spirits. The defense of the championship had officially begun.

CHAPTER TWO

Practice Makes Perfect

On the first Saturday of the season, the players attended a Knoxville basketball clinic for high school and college coaches instead of the regular practice. Sponsored by Converse and the Women's Basketball Coaches Association, the clinic was one of eight sessions held around the country in the fall of 1987. Each clinic featured such well-known coaches as Jody Conradt of Texas; Kay Yow of North Carolina State; Linda Sharp of the University of Southern California; Sue Gunter of Louisiana State University; Jane Albright of Northern Illinois University; Sylvia Hatchell of the University of North Carolina, Chapel Hill; and Joe Ciampi of Auburn. These mentors spoke on various topics, and collegiate squads from local campuses demonstrated drills and strategies. NCAA representatives were on hand to respond to questions regarding recruiting regulations.

At the Knoxville clinic, Van Chancellor of the University of Mississippi lectured the assembled coaches in the morning. Coach Summitt took over in the afternoon. By virtue of her contract with Converse, Summitt would make three additional appearances during the season to represent the shoe company.

For their $40 registration fee, coaches attending the clinic received a packet of clinic notes including detailed Xs and Os of the material in the lectures. They were also given the first issue of *Coaching Women's Basketball*, the official journal of the Women's Basketball Coaches Association. This issue featured the Lady Volunteer coach and assistant Mickie DeMoss on the cover. It also included an article on "Tennessee's Preseason Conditioning Program." One of its authors, Whitey Hitchcock, was a doctoral candidate in exercise physiology at the University of Tennessee, Knoxville (UTK), and had been the conditioning coach for the women's basketball team for 3 years.

When it was Pat's turn to speak, the audience of about 200 coaches listened intently. Pat began her lecture by stressing the importance of planning. Before and after each practice session, she explained, she and her assistants determined what aspects of the game needed attention and developed strategies to help individual players work on their weaknesses. Based on these discussions, the head coach brought a written outline to each practice and referred to it as the workout progressed. Variety is also essential, she said. Varying drills relieves boredom and helps develop concentration.

As team members demonstrated drills, Pat yelled encouragement, stopped to make corrections, and did not hesitate to reprimand players who were not performing to her expectations. A few coaches in the audience were obviously taken aback when Summitt shouted at her senior post player, Kathy Spinks, "Kathy, don't miss those easy shots! Concentrate!"

But Kathy, obviously accustomed to such directives, just answered "Rebound." Kathy, a 6-2, 170-pound forward, was a big, wholesome kid who was not a natural athlete but made up for lack of speed and agility with hustle, determination, and strength. In that way, she reminded Pat of herself, and there was an obvious affection between them. In Kathy's 4 years at Tennessee, Pat had gotten to know the Kentucky native well, and Kathy had learned to trust Pat and to accept her criticism gracefully.

Throughout the demonstration, coaches asked Pat questions, which she answered in great detail, often using players to illustrate her responses. By the end of the afternoon, the players were as sweat-drenched as after a normal practice.

On Monday, players were back in Stokely Athletics Center. For the first week of practice, Summitt had been patient with the rookies, but by the second week there was a drastic change. "Pearl, you're too smart to be taking so long to learn this!'' she shouted. "Get with it!'' To Durham, she yelled, "Dadgummit, Kris, pay attention!'' Both seemed to take the criticism well, but Summitt kept complaining that Kris was not demonstrating enough intensity. Still, she interspersed her criticisms with, "Good hustle, Pearl, good hustle'' or, after an exceptional pass, "Good look, Kris, good look.''

Teammates were, for the most part, tolerant when the freshmen missed assignments or made other rookie mistakes. Occasionally there was a look of disgust at Pearl when the 6-4 forward failed to catch an easy pass and thus missed a chance at a basket. Mostly, players were helpful and supportive of one another. Bridgette Gordon, for example, tactfully spoke to Pat in private to tell her that Pearl was positioning herself incorrectly on a particular defensive drill. Pat then stopped the practice and demonstrated the correct technique.

One day during the second week, Pat and the assistants were late to practice. The team formed their usual circle to stretch. Suddenly Lisa Webb, the 5-9 senior forward from Georgia, drawled, "Pearl, you farted!'' With that announcement, all the Tennessee players howled with laughter and moved away from the embarrassed freshman. Then someone came to Pearl's defense. "Lisa, you have no room to talk. Remember when you bent over to pick up a book in class the other day and let a big one?'' More howls of laughter.

At this point the head coach entered. Since the two freshmen had yet to see Summitt smile at a practice, they squirmed uneasily. But when Summitt saw the rest of the team rolling on the floor, she looked at her manager, Laura Craig, and said two words: "Gas—Pearl.'' Craig nodded, and for the first time in 2 weeks, Summitt broke into a broad grin. Then she admonished the team, "Quit abusing Pearl. She gets enough abuse from me.'' More laughter.

Rather than starting practice right away, Summitt called the team over and sat with them on the floor to read a card she had received from Shelia Collins, the former Lady Vol who was playing basketball in Germany. Many of the players knew Shelia, since she had graduated just 2 years before. Shelia wrote that her team played a game in Budapest and that she was named the most valuable player.

Then Pat produced from the pocket of her warm-up a jeweler's mock-up of the medal the players were to receive for having won the national championship. It was a small, round piece of jewelry that could be worn as a necklace. The mock-up was in bronze, but the final product would be gold. The medal had "NCAA'' and a "1'' on the front; on the back were the score and the date of the championship. Team members passed the medal around the circle, obviously impressed. Kris and Pearl feigned disinterest since they were not a part of the championship team, but Summitt insisted that they examine the prize. Holding the tangible evidence of a national championship, Summitt wagered, would be a potent motivator for any athlete.

There followed some discussion of what type of chain would look best with the medal. Dawn Marsh volunteered to check prices at a local jeweler, since players would have to purchase their own chains.

When practice began, a new team cohesion was evident. The teasing with Pearl had created a congenial, family atmosphere, and the card from Shelia Collins reinforced that sentiment, holding out a promise of life after college basketball. The championship necklace reminded the athletes of the exhilaration of being members of a successful national team.

1987-88 Lady Vol players and coaching staff: *1st row L to R.* Lisa Webb, 34; Dawn Marsh, 4; Tonya Edwards, 33; Kris Durham, 23; Melissa McCray, 35. *2nd row.* Shelley Sexton, Mickie DeMoss, Pat Summitt, Holly Warlick, Heidi Van Derveer. *3rd row.* Jennifer Tuggle, 32; Carla McGhee, 24; Sheila Frost, 12; Pearl Moore, 42; Kathy Spinks, 11; Bridgette Gordon, 30.

In the middle of the second week of practice, Kerry Howland, the academic advisor for women's athletics, came to the gym and gave progress cards to all the players. The women received a card for every class in which they were enrolled, and were instructed to give them to their professors. The professors were to report the athlete's academic progress, attitude, and attendance, sign the card, and return it to Howland.

No one spoke her name, but when Howland showed up the players couldn't help but think of Daedra Charles, the Michigan freshman who would be forced to sit out this year because of the new NCAA academic requirement known as Proposition 48. Prop 48 mandated that incoming freshmen must score at least 700 on their combined SATs or 15 on their composite ACTs to be eligible for play; Daedra Charles was Tennessee's first frosh not to make the grade, and her absence was painfully conspicuous.

In the 14 years of Summitt's tenure at Tennessee, all of her athletes who had played 4 years had graduated. But with the new, more stringent NCAA requirements for admission and retention, emphasis on academic performance had increased. All of the freshmen, plus any Lady Vols who did not have a 2.5 grade point average, would be required to attend study hall in a designated room in Stokely Athletics Center from 4:00 to 6:30 p.m. daily. When the 2.5 was reached or the freshman year over, the study hall requirement would be dropped. For athletes requiring help, tutors would be provided.

Kerry Howland was a former Tennessee swimmer. As academic advisor for all 90 women athletes, Kerry had responsibilities including making sure the athletes were properly registered, monitoring players' academic progress, and explaining entrance and eligibility requirements to potential recruits. Howland studied transcripts and worked with guidance counselors, parents, and athletes to ensure that all requirements were met. The staff of Tennessee's women's athletic department was determined that its athletes would not mimic the abysmal graduation rate of male college athletes.

Most of the players seemed equally determined. In the previous season, Kathy Spinks had even taken 2 weeks off from basketball to devote more time to her studies. She had started the first 10 games of the season, but in late January she asked Coach Summitt for time off to study, and Summitt, in a move uncharacteristic of any college coach, granted her request. Spinks missed 2 weeks of practice and the road trips to Northwestern and Louisiana Tech. By early March she had regained her playing form, and helped her team win the championship. Her studying also paid off: She made the dean's list for the first time. At the end of this year, she would be the first person in her family to graduate from college.

On Friday and Saturday of the second week of practice, the team entertained Vicki Hall, a sought-after recruit from Indianapolis. Summitt and her two assistant coaches flew to Indianapolis on Friday morning and brought Vicki back with them, making Hall the first female recruit to have been flown to the Knoxville campus on a UTK plane. Since NCAA rules forbid coaches to give parents extra benefits when their child is being recruited, Mr. and Mrs. Hall drove to Knoxville.

While on campus, Hall would have private meetings with Dr. Edward Boling, President of the university; Dr. Joan Paul, head of the department of physical education and dance; academic advisor Kerry Howland; and Tina Buckles, the sport psychologist who volunteered her services to the Lady Vol athletic program. Not all recruits who make official visits to Tennessee meet with the UTK president, but all prospects do meet with Howland and a representative of the academic department of their choice. Since Vicki was planning to become a sport psychologist, she was scheduled to meet with Buckles.

An excellent student (with a 3.8 grade point average out of a possible 4.0), as well as an exceptional athlete, Hall was a most appealing recruit. Beginning in her junior year, she and her mother had been answering 7 to 10 calls per day from interested college coaches. Mrs. Hall had grown particularly fond of Andy Landers, the Georgia coach, with whom she had talked on many occasions. Apparently the daughter did not share her mother's sentiments, since Vicki had narrowed her choices to three schools: Tennessee, Texas, and Iowa.

After her arrival at the Knoxville airport, Vicki and the coaches rushed to get to Stokely Athletics Center in time for the 12:15 p.m. practice. When the trio arrived at the gymnasium, the team was already seated in the standard circle performing stretching exercises. Hanging prominently from a balcony was a large hand-printed sign, WELCOME VICKI HALL.

Pat made the introductions and Kris Durham, who had played on a national team with Vicki that past summer, welcomed the prize recruit with a hug. Tonya Edwards had been Vicki's teammate the previous summer on the Jones Cup squad, which won the gold medal in Taipei, Taiwan, and Bridgette Gordon and Sheila Frost had also competed with Vicki at the Pan American tryouts the previous summer. They all greeted her warmly. Their camaraderie was evident by black Bridgette's joke to blonde Vicki, "If you come to Tennessee, you are going to have to spend a lot of time in a tanning salon."

When Friday's practice began, drills were as strenuous as always, and Pat reprimanded at her usual volume. Most of the time, Summitt appeared oblivious to Hall, who sat quietly on the sidelines.

Fifteen minutes before the usual dismissal time, Coach Summitt instructed Dawn Marsh to shoot a free throw. "If you make it, Dawn, practice is over," she told her. "If you miss, we continue to work." Amid cheers from her teammates, Marsh stepped to the free throw line and calmly sank the shot. All the players cheered. Vicki Hall remained impassive.

Saturday's practice was from 8:00 to 10:00 in the morning. The men would practice after the women, then both teams would meet for a barbecue lunch. Don DeVoe's team was also entertaining two recruits that weekend, and he and Pat agreed a get-together would enhance the recruiting effort. After lunch the recruits, most of the Tennessee athletes, and 93,000 other fans would attend the Tennessee–Georgia Tech football game in Neyland Stadium.

At practice that Saturday, the Lady Vols were sluggish. Hall, watching from the sidelines, appeared bored with the whole scene. Her parents, sitting on the opposite side of Stokely, seemed much more enthusiastic than their talented daughter.

The tempo of the practice picked up as Pat's yelling increased. Fans arriving early for the football game began strolling into Stokely to watch the defending national champions in action, and the presence of more spectators provided the squad with an added incentive to perform.

At about 9:00 Donna Fielden, one of a handful of women officials in the area, arrived to explain minor rule changes relating to the three-point shot and intentional fouls. She also noted that for the first time the NCAA had published one rule book for both women and men. The book delineated the slight differences between the men's and women's games, but Fielden emphasized that they were essentially the same.

Next, the players scrimmaged for 20 minutes, one squad coached by Holly Warlick, the other by Mickie DeMoss. Summitt observed from the sidelines, seated next to Hall. From her spectator's position, the head coach did not hesitate to offer her opinion of the play. Still no reaction from Hall.

After practice, Summitt singled out Bridgette Gordon, Jennifer Tuggle, Lisa Webb, and Dawn Marsh for special commendation. Dawn's passing had been phenomenal, and Jennifer and Lisa had benefited from the summer's weight-training program. Bridgette Gordon had become a team leader

Number 30 Bridgette Gordon vs. LSU

by example, hustling at every practice and maintaining the intensity level Summitt demanded.

What Coach Summitt didn't say was that the belligerence and laziness that characterized Bridgette's first 2 years had disappeared. Shy and defiant as a freshman, the tall forward had rarely taken her eyes off the floor. Now she held her head high and occasionally smiled, revealing straight white teeth. One of the smartest players on the team, Gordon was now asking good questions and offering insightful suggestions about strategy. She hadn't received the star treatment that she had expected from Summitt and would have received from some other coaches, but she seemed to have adjusted. Already she was considered one of the best players in the country. With this new maturity, what might she be able to accomplish now? Summitt's hopes were high.

Pat then asked student assistant Shelley Sexton for her impressions of the team. The captain of last year's national championship team, Shelley had returned this year to help coach while finishing her degree in sport management. Shelley used the opportunity to praise the freshmen. "Kris and Pearl have picked up the system better and more quickly, and they work harder at conditioning, than any freshmen I've seen at Tennessee," she said. But she added, "I'm concerned about the pressure of being defending national champions. We must play one game at a time. If we concentrate on trying to repeat last year's success, the pressure will most likely cause a collapse due to, among other things, burnout."

As the team filed out of Stokely Gym on this weather-perfect fall morning, they did not seem concerned about burnout. There would be no Sunday practice, they had a barbecue to look forward to, and they were still the Number 1 team in women's basketball.

CHAPTER THREE

The Shape of Things to Come

After last year's championship, each athlete had met with Whitey Hitchcock, the conditioning coach, to establish strength, speed, and endurance goals for the following year. Hitchcock was a graduate assistant at UTK whose responsibilities included working half-time as the strength and conditioning coach in women's athletics and half-time teaching physical education classes. He and the athletes also discussed body weight to determine whether the athlete was competing at what she and the conditioning coach considered "ideal playing weight." Whitey then developed a summer workout program for each member of the team.

In consultation with Coach Summitt, Whitey had determined team goals. For example, the goal for average body fat was 17 percent. "In the general population," Hitchcock says, "average body fat for females is 15 to 25 percent, so we don't feel 17 percent is unreasonable, but knowing the athlete is important. You have to know when to demand and when to back off."

Other team goals included being able to run the mile and one-half in 10 minutes and 30 seconds for the wing players and 11 minutes for the post players, bench-press at least 75 percent of body weight, and squat-lift 1.5 times body weight.

Jennifer Tuggle had asked Whitey if he would work with her over the summer since both would be on campus for summer school. Jennifer, a math and business major who had attended Lady Vol games as a child and always dreamed of being a Lady Vol, was not having the kind of career she had hoped for. After the knee injury in her sophomore year, she had played very little. Whitey agreed to help Jennifer on the condition that she work hard, and she kept her part of the bargain, training 3 days a week for 8 weeks and never showing up late for a workout.

They did have a few conflicts, though. "I hate it when people try to motivate me," Jennifer would say.

Whitey's response: "I'll keep yelling, you keep ignoring, and I won't take it personally."

Eventually, Tuggle increased her vertical jump by 4 inches, made the distance run standard on her first attempt (she ran it in 10:45, the first post player to meet the 11-minute standard), and was able to bench-press her goal of 100 pounds. Last year her maximum had been 85.

"Jennifer worked her butt off," reports Hitchcock. "I have tremendous respect for Jennifer Tuggle."

Lisa Webb was another of Whitey's success stories. At 5-9, Webb thrilled fans and teammates by leaping over taller players to grab rebounds, and had played guard, forward, and even center in her freshman year. But like Tuggle, she had had knee surgery, and she had received an artificial ligament in her sophomore season. Her junior season was a slow year.

Now, as a senior, her weight was 159, down from last year's 165; she had increased her weight lifting by 30 percent to 155 in the bench press and 275 in the squat lift; she ran 40 yards in 5.3 seconds and had a vertical jump of 26 inches. The former high school homecoming queen was ready to strut her stuff.

Whitey also had high hopes for Kris Durham. Kris had come to the university for summer orientation and, after being tested by Whitey, was given an individualized conditioning program. Whitey found that Kris had muscle bulk, but lacked strength. Kris's previous weight-lifting program had not addressed her specific strength needs, so Whitey adjusted it. When she reported in September for prepractice conditioning, she was stronger and several pounds lighter. Said Whitey, "Kris, I hope, will be like Dawn, developing from a slow, chunky white kid to a lean, fast college athlete."

Number 32 Jennifer Tuggle vs. Florida

Dawn had indeed developed into a well-conditioned basketball player. As a senior, she was the fastest and best-conditioned of any Lady Vol. She ran the mile and one-half in 9:55, faster than any of her teammates. Her vertical jump was 22 inches; she bench-pressed 115 and squat-lifted 185. Her 40-yard dash of 5.2 seconds was also the best on her team. During high school and up until her junior year she weighed 131, but by her senior year she had reduced that to 128. Three pounds may seem insignificant, but Whitey believed that at this level of competition, it made a difference in terms of quickness.

The preseason conditioning program had lasted about 4 weeks, up until the opening of regular practice on October 15. Team members ran on the track 2 days per week and lifted weights the other 3. They also did jumping and agility drills. Whitey worked closely with Pat to determine the kinds of workouts needed once the actual season began.

Working for Pat, Whitey said, was an invaluable experience. "If I ever had concerns about working for a woman, those have all been dispelled. I have learned a tremendous amount from Pat, and if I ever have trouble working for a female, I'll know it's because she is a sorry supervisor and not because of her gender and not because of my chauvinistic hang-ups."

As the first road trip, the Communiplex Classic offered the players a chance to begin to come together as a team. There were just 10 of them now—5 black and 5 white—and already they felt like friends. They also felt like survivors, aware of their privileged status. Freshman Daedra Charles had been deemed academically ineligible, Carla McGhee was going to be out for the season because of the car accident, Karla Horton had opted for marriage over basketball (an unfathomable choice to the current players), and last year's walk-on, Gay Townsend, had walked off. In the previous year, Townsend had played in 10 games, but for a total of only 16 minutes. So, after participating in preseason practice, the physical education major decided to play intramural basketball instead.

Still, Gay's friendships with the players, especially her roommate, Lisa Webb, remained strong. Relationships among other team members were also good. Lisa and Melissa McCray were becoming team leaders, and, with Tonya Edwards, formed a frequent trio. Sheila Frost had asked the head manager, Laura Craig, and Laura's roommate to live with her. Shelley Sexton, the popular captain of last year's squad, was still around, this year as a student assistant coach. Kris Durham and Pearl Moore, the two freshmen, had become buddies.

Because the squad was small, because they were all good, and because they knew Pat's coaching style included lots of substitutions, none of the team members feared a bench-sitting season like the walk-on Gay Townsend's. There was nervousness and competitiveness, but so far, there were no personality conflicts, and much to everyone's relief, no apparent black-white tensions.

Nevertheless, it was probably inspirational for Tennessee's five black athletes—Lisa, Melissa, Tonya, Pearl, and Bridgette—that the 1987-88 season opened with a tournament sponsored by Communiplex Services, Inc., a minority-owned business in Cincinnati, Ohio. The president, Steven Reece, had initiated the Communiplex National Hall of Fame Basketball Classic in 1984, and the following year established the Women's Sports Hall of Fame in Cincinnati. Reece and his staff served as excellent role models for the young athletes.

Since 1985 a luncheon has been held in conjunction with the basketball tournament to induct into the Hall of Fame individuals who have contributed significantly to women's athletics. Pat Head Summitt had been so honored at the inaugural luncheon. This year, Wilma Rudolf, also one of the original inductees, presented the 1987 awards. Inductees included Vivian Stringer, the head basketball coach at the University of Iowa and one of the few black female head coaches; Donna Lopiano, athletic director at the University of Texas; Anita DeFrantz, Olympic rower and member of the International Olympic Committee; Donna Cheek, the first black equestrian to represent the United States in Olympic competition (1984); Margo Schott, owner of the Cincinnati Reds baseball team; and Ed Temple, famed Olympic track coach and head coach of the Tigerbelles at Tennessee State University.

The Communiplex Classic itself was disappointing. Games were played at a local technical college, in an antiquated gymnasium with a seating capacity of 1,800. The largest crowd was estimated at 1,233, and only about 900 people attended the championship game. Media coverage was also dismal. The two Knoxville papers and the Nashville *Tennessean* sent reporters, but there was little coverage in Cincinnati and no national exposure. One had to wonder what the situation would have been had Indiana, the defending men's champion, been playing in the tournament.

The competition among the four teams did nothing to add excitement. The opening game, between Old Dominion and the University of Cincinnati, was characterized by sloppy passing and poor shooting; clearly the early season kinks were not yet ironed out. Old Dominion finally won, 59-49. In the second game, which began at the awful hour of 9:30 p.m., Tennessee overwhelmed Indiana, 91-52.

The next day, Old Dominion defeated Indiana in a closer match. Apparently Bobby Knight's antics were not contagious, and Jorja Hoehn, the coach of the Hoosiers' women's team, was gracious in defeat. However, she did leave immediately after the game rather than staying for the awards ceremony.

UTK and Old Dominion played in the championship game, again at 9:30 p.m. "Old Dominion did not come to this tournament to play Cincinnati," Coach Summitt told her team. "They came to play Tennessee." That was clear from the opening minutes, when Donna Harrington, ODU's 6-2 forward, scored from all over the court while Tennessee players watched her in awe. By halftime, however, Tennessee had regained control of themselves and commanded an 11-point lead. The second half degenerated into a game of brute force. Poor James Naismith, who invented this "non-contact" sport in 1891, was probably turning over in his grave. Bodies banged into each other and players groaned loudly. Harrington knocked 6-4 Sheila Frost to the floor on several occasions. "Take the charge!" yelled Summitt to her post player.

"If Frost takes one more charge, they are going to have to take her out on a stretcher," commented a spectator.

But it was difficult for Sheila Frost to stand her ground. Noncombative by nature, Sheila was more inclined to back up a step, if not step aside altogether, when Harrington, only 2 inches shorter and several pounds heavier, ran toward her. The youngest of five children and the second shortest, Sheila had been nicknamed "PeeWee" by her family, but Summitt hated the term and banished it from the Lady Vol vocabulary. "You should play like you're 6-8!" Summitt would yell. "You should be dominating! Stand your ground!"

Eventually Tennessee prevailed, 83-52, Bridgette Gordon and Dawn Marsh were named to the all-tournament team, and Gordon was named most valuable player. What a difference from the opening of the 1986 season, when Gordon did not even start in several games because her performance did not meet Pat's standards.

Apparently Summitt was using the same tactic to motivate sophomore guard Tonya Edwards. As a rookie the previous year, Tonya had walked away with MVP honors at the NCAA championship. Nicknamed "Ice," Tonya was especially cool at the free throw line, sinking 89 of 113 the previous year, the most in the Southeastern Conference and the best percentage (79 percent) of her team. But Tonya did not start in either game in

Number 12 Sheila Frost vs. Florida

the Communiplex tournament. She did play well coming off the bench, scoring 11 points in the first game and 15 against ODU.

For the players, the Cincinnati trip offered a chance to shake out their early season jitters, to honor athletes who had come before them, and to begin to gel as a team. For interested observers, the Communiplex Classic trip brought forth a telling anecdote about Pat Head Summitt, related by a Lady Vol booster who asked not to be named.

A great fan of Tennessee, this woman drove her truck more than 250 miles to Ohio to watch her favorite team kick off the season. She stayed in the same hotel as the team, and Pat invited her to ride the team bus to and from the games. In return for this courtesy, Summitt asked the booster if she would transport one of the managers to a local laundromat to wash the players' socks before the championship game.

More than willing to oblige, the Lady Vol supporter asked the doorman to have her truck brought to the hotel entrance. When the truck finally arrived, the manager and booster hopped in. But it was pouring rain, the Saturday night traffic was terrible, and though they drove for 30 minutes, they never found the laundromat. Finally, in frustration, they returned to the hotel where the bellhop had the socks washed, free of charge, in the hotel laundry facility.

Mission accomplished, the booster sent her truck back to the garage. She then returned to her room to wait for the team bus. Originally the team bus was to have left at 8:15, but the booster overheard Pat tell the driver that, since the socks had to be washed, they would not leave until 8:30. When the exhausted booster arrived at 8:20 to board, she discovered they had left without her. Fortunately she spotted a sportswriter from Knoxville who gave her a ride to the game. She was grateful for the lift, since it spared her the odyssey of retrieving her truck and trying to find the Cincinnati Technical College Gymnasium, across town from the hotel.

At first, the booster was angry at Pat for having left without her. Then she remembered what had happened to R.B. Summitt, Pat's husband. The night before, Pat had returned with her coaching staff to the hotel to watch game films instead of joining her spouse and the rest of the team for a postgame meal. R.B. was left to enjoy the late-night supper with the Lady Vol team minus the Lady Vol coach. At least, thought the booster, Pat treats everyone the same.

Pat and Ralph Barnes Summitt II (R.B.) met in April 1977. At the time, R.B. was working as a state bank examiner, and Marsha McGreager, Pat's roommate and one of R.B.'s co-workers, introduced them. They dated more than 3 years before marrying on August 23, 1980. The reason for the long courtship, Pat explains, was "so we could make sure that we could handle a two-career marriage and that R.B. could adjust to my hectic schedule."

After 8 years, R.B. remains extremely supportive of Pat's team and the Lady Vol athletic program in general. He attends all home games and as many away contests as his job will permit. He frequently accompanies Pat on her speaking engagements and is usually present when she receives her awards.

R.B.'s job is also demanding. He is chairman of the board and executive vice president of Sevier County Bank; his father is the president. According to Pat, "working for one's father is always a special challenge, but R.B. manages this well and has become very successful in his own right." Pat attributes much of her husband's success to his being "highly intelligent."

Pat and R.B. live in Seymour, about 15 miles south of Knoxville. Each owned a house when they were married, but R.B. sold his and moved in with Pat. While they were on their honeymoon, he had a deck built on the back of the house. When they returned, the new bride was delighted with the surprise addition. Last year they added a swimming pool, and both enjoy swimming, sunbathing, and admiring their view of the Smoky Mountains.

When they were first married, the young couple frequently played racquetball together, but they became too competitive, trying to defeat each other, and decided it was not good for their marriage. They began a running program, but R.B. has recently been bothered by an old hip injury and has resigned himself to swimming for exercise. Pat still manages to run about 3 miles several times each week.

Though Pat has no intention of retiring any time soon, she is trying to make more time for her marriage by cutting back on public speaking engagements. "Of course," says Pat, "R.B. and I sometimes get frustrated with our hectic lifestyles and the conflicts that are bound to occur with a two-career marriage. But I think we have adjusted to it pretty well."

The first official function to be held in the Thompson-Boling Assembly Center and Arena—otherwise known as "the arena"—was a doubleheader basketball game on December 3, 1987. The Lady Vols played Stetson University and the Gentlemen Vols played Marquette. The women's game and the arena were both subject to considerable controversy—the game because fans resented the women's having to play preliminary to the men and the arena because of problems involved in construction of the facility.

Scheduling doubleheader basketball games had never been popular among certain women's basketball supporters. According to them, playing preliminary to the men gave the impression that the women's game was less important. In the case of the Lady Vols, there were even more compelling arguments against doubleheaders: They were expensive and seat assignments for the women's game were terrible.

For the men's games, doubleheaders were included in the $138 price of a season ticket, and holders of season tickets sat in the same reserved seat for both single and double games. Lady Vol season subscribers, on the other hand, had to buy two sets of tickets, one for the single games costing $50 and, for an additional $50, a five-game doubleheader package. People buying both sets of tickets were assigned two different seats. For single Lady Vol games, the seats were on the first level, close to the floor, but for the doubleheaders, fans were removed from the action to the second and third tiers.

Advocates of the doubleheaders defended their position by maintaining that women's basketball in general would benefit from the exposure, and that the Lady Vol program would benefit from the increased revenue. In terms of exposure, the thinking was that many of the men's fans had not seen a women's game, and that some of those fans would, perhaps by arriving a little early, witness a great competition and become loyal supporters of the women as well.

Exposure is arguable; money is not. By playing preliminary to the men, the women would receive $2 of each ticket sold. That is substantial revenue, since 13,000 season tickets were sold to men's games. When individual game tickets were added, the Lady Vols stood to gain a conservative estimate of $150,000 for the five doubleheaders ($2 per ticket × 15,000 fans × 5 games).

In spite of the financial benefits, the doubleheaders had caused such grief for longtime Lady Vol supporters, who had in turn caused such grief for women's athletic director Joan Cronan, that Cronan was considering discontinuing this format the following year. The Boost-Her Club had been particularly upset with the arrangement, and Cronan was concerned about losing their support. She did make clear, however, that the task of raising an extra $150,000 would then fall on the Boost-Hers.

The building of the arena itself was the source of heated debate between those supporting athletics and those who opposed what they called the

Number 33 Tonya Edwards vs. Stetson

"jockocracy." Those favoring athletics saw the arena as a necessity, not only to satisfy ticket demands but also to recruit quality athletes. Proponents maintained that UTK's Stokely Center was outdated, and that without the new facility, Tennessee would not be able to compete with other Southeastern Conference schools.

Opponents of the arena were particularly vocal. The Faculty Senate, the UTK chapter of the American Association of University Professors, and the president of the Student Government Association all opposed the project. When their advice was ignored, 86 UTK professors filed suit against the university, the public building authority, Knox county, and the city of Knoxville, challenging the financial scheme of the proposed $30 million structure. The financial package included $7 million from the state (the $7 million had already been appropriated for a no-longer-needed state office building in Knoxville, and unless the money was used immediately, according to university officials, it would be reabsorbed by the state); $10 million from Knox County; $3 million from UTK revenues such as ticket sales and arena parking fees; $5 million from matching gifts; and a $5 million gift from B. Ray Thompson, for whom the building was eventually named, along with university president Edward J. Boling.

The concern of the faculty was that this complicated funding plan would divert academic monies to the athletic facility. They argued that there was a much greater need for a new library.

The lawsuit was settled in April 1983, when professors signed an agreement that specified, among other things, that the men's athletic department budget would have to be completely depleted before any university funds would be spent to construct the facility. Depleting the athletic department budget at UTK is akin to depleting Fort Knox, so the faculty were amenable to this condition. The court also ordered the university to make full disclosures, upon request, to the Faculty Senate of the funding and operation of the arena.

This minor victory was celebrated in academic circles, but there was even greater rejoicing when the state appropriated $30 million for renovation of the Hodges Library. Ironically, the Hodges Library renovation was completed on time and the library opened for business in September 1987, preceding arena occupancy by 3 months. So in the brains-versus-brawn competition symbolized by the two structures, brains had won in terms of speed and brawn was victorious in terms of its right to exist.

But the arena was plagued by two other lawsuits. In 1985, B.B. Anderson, the original contractor, sued the university, charging that UTK's engineering and design team was responsible for costly delays. In 1987 the university filed a $107 million countersuit charging breach of contract. At this writing, the suit is still pending.

In addition to the court proceedings, the arena was often in the Knoxville news because of the contention that the structure was unsafe since it was built on top of underground caves. There was so much news coverage over the 6-year period that the facility itself almost became more interesting than the teams for which it was built. As Marshall McLuhan pointed out in the late sixties, the medium had become more important than the message.

On opening night, December 3, 1987, both Tennessee teams won their games. The women defeated Stetson 102-59, and the men defeated Marquette 82-56. Dawn Marsh scored the first two points in the arena, and Tonya Edwards scored the arena's first three-pointer, launching the ball in the final seconds to put the Vols over the century mark.

Press reports contained little about basketball games. They noted that vandals had stuffed toilets with paper cups and caused substantial flooding in the new arena, and they cited an amusing account about a mouse that had attended the postgame press conference and allegedly frightened one of the Stetson women players. Mostly they quoted the fans (12,300 by the end of the women's game; 24,535 for the men), many of whom were eager to share their lavish praise for the new arena.

CHAPTER FOUR

Of Haylofts and Hoops

Patricia Sue Head was born in Clarksville, Tennessee, on June 14, 1952, to farmers Hazel and Richard Head. Harry Truman was president, *Time* magazine sold for 20 cents a copy, and for $158.85, United Airlines flew passengers from New York to San Francisco in 11 hours and 35 minutes.

The year Patricia was born, the Heads already had three young sons: 7-year-old Tommy, 4-year-old Charles, and 2-year-old Kenneth. Pat, known as Trish to her family, pitched in with the farmwork as soon as she could, driving a tractor and plowing the tobacco field by the time she was 11. She also milked the cows, rode horses, set tobacco, and would often embarrass her brothers by throwing bales of hay higher than they could.

Pat also raised her own calf every year as a 4-H Club project. Though many youngsters would consider taking care of an animal a chore, Pat loved it. Jane Brown Clark, Pat's best friend then and now, remembers that the two of them returned to the Head residence from a double date around midnight one cold winter's night. They had just gotten in bed when Pat remembered she had not watered her calf. She begged Jane to go with her to the barn where, due to a frozen pipe, there was no water. Pat, ever resourceful, went back to the house, and with Jane's help dragged a hose across the road to the barn where the thirsty baby calf finally was given a drink. The animal had to drink fast, though, because it was so cold that the water froze almost as soon as it left the hose. That experience convinced Jane, a city kid, that life on the farm was not for sissies.

Unlike her brothers, Pat was expected to work inside as well as outside. She helped her mother with the household chores while her father, according to Pat, "treated me like another son." She told a story to illustrate her point: "Once when I was plowing, the blade on the plow broke and I sent for my dad to come fix it. When he got there, he was furious and wanted to know why I hadn't fixed it myself. You better believe I never sent for him again. The next time a blade broke, I figured out for myself how to fix the thing." Added Pat, "I always feared my dad. He was a stern, strong disciplinarian. A man of few words, but very opinionated."

Pat was an admirer of her oldest brother, Tommy, who was a basketball standout in high school, then at Austin Peay State University in Clarksville. Probably more than any other factor, Tommy's example inspired his sister's future success. Hour after hour, day after day, Tommy and Pat played two-on-two against Charles and Kenneth on a makeshift court in the barn. Pat and Tommy often won. Explains Pat, "As Tommy got better, they would double-team him, and I learned to shoot."

Those games are some of Pat's fondest memories of her childhood. She still contends that a hayloft in a big barn makes a wonderful basketball court: almost regulation in size, though not quite as wide as it should be. Her dad even installed lights so the kids could play after supper when the chores were finished. So what if their court was sometimes strewn with hay? Such obstacles never stop true lovers of the sport.

When Pat was six, her parents had another daughter, Linda, but since Linda was so much younger than her brothers, she never had the opportunity to play basketball with them. She did play some with Pat, and played varsity ball in high school, but never shared her family's passion for the sport.

Richard Head is almost fanatical about the game. He hates to lose, and is particularly agitated nowadays when Pat's Lady Vols lose. Hazel

Head is the opposite: even-tempered and philosophical about defeat. "Mom knows losing a basketball game isn't the worst thing that can happen to a person," says Pat. "She keeps it in perspective."

"Miss Hazel," as she is affectionately known by people in the community, is soft-spoken, caring, and neighborly. In Pat's words, "My mom is the hardest worker I have ever seen. She's often up at 5:00 in the morning to work in the garden, always cooks three huge delicious meals a day, and at night will string well over a bushel and a half of beans while watching television." Like her daughter, Hazel Head also does "outside work," mowing the huge lawn around the family homestead and helping Richard in his various businesses.

Pat's father is a jack-of-all-trades. He has been a farmer and a contractor, and has owned a feed store, a grocery store, and a hardware store. Now semiretired, he runs a tobacco warehouse in Springfield, Tennessee.

Gloria Ray, former women's athletic director at UTK and a close friend of Pat's, offers this insight into the relationship between Pat and her parents. "Pat is a perfect clone of her father. She disciplines her players the way her father disciplined her. Fortunately, Pat has a lot of Hazel in her, too: She's a warm, caring, people-person. Pat can use that when she thinks a player needs it. I believe Pat is still trying to please her dad, but she enjoys from her mom an unconditional love. Hazel loves her even when she finishes third!"

Pat agrees with Gloria, adding, "My dad has never hugged me or said he loved me. But I know he's proud of me."

Pat Head's competitive basketball career began when she was nine. In seventh grade she suffered a minor setback when, in an attempt to touch the basketball net, she leapt off the school gymnasium/auditorium stage and broke her arm. Terribly disappointed over not being able to play, 12-year-old Pat soaked the cast in water and chipped away at the plaster so she could bend her elbow enough to practice shooting. Apparently this did not interfere with the healing process, and by the next season, she led her team in scoring.

That year, her eighth-grade team went undefeated and "Bone" Head was named most valuable player in the elementary tournament. Pictures of Pat on that team reveal a tall, skinny girl with curly brown hair, intent eyes, and a broad smile.

By the time she completed the eighth grade, "Bone" Head was no longer a descriptive nickname. Pat laughed about it recently. "I can't believe it, but I kept putting on weight until at one time in college, I weighed 165."

When it came time for high school, Pat's classmates proceeded from Roosevelt Elementary to Clarksville High School. But Clarksville High did not have a girl's basketball team. The year was 1966, before Title IX, before athletic scholarships for women, before Olympic women's basketball, and before any hint of a pro league for women. But for Pat to continue playing the sport she had come to love, the Head family moved the short distance from Montgomery to Cheatham County so Pat could attend Cheatham County High School in Ashland City. After Pat's high school career, Hazel and Richard Head remained in Henrietta, Tennessee, the unincorporated community between Ashland City and Clarksville.

By her freshman year, Pat had reached her full height of 5-10 and weighed 135 pounds. Mike Jarreau, the coach, did not generally start a freshman on the varsity squad, but Pat's size and raw talent secured her a spot as a forward on the starting six (the girls' game in those days was played with three forwards and three guards on a split court).

Even after all her later success, Pat still regrets that her high school team never made it to the state tournament. She remembers vividly that day in 1970 when Cheatham County High School was eliminated from the regional tournament: "Gracie Oliver played at Hendersonville and she was great. We lost to them in the semifinals of the regionals, and I cried and cried. I was a senior, and it was my last chance to get to play in a state tournament. I was still crying when I got in the front seat of the car with my dad for the drive home. He was so mad at me, and, of course, as disappointed as I was about the loss. I remember that he called me a baby and said if I didn't stop sniffling that when we got home he was going to give me something to cry about."

Pat recalls another high school game with a happier ending. It was against Springfield High School and went into five overtimes. Pat's team won when Norma Gibbs, a left-handed forward who hadn't taken a shot all night, made the winning basket. Thinking back to the long-ago game, Pat said, "I loved it. Can you imagine five overtimes? The pressure was awesome, and then one of the lesser-known players was the hero. It was great."

Pat had an outstanding senior season. She scored 40 or more points twice; one journalist described her as a "fierce, intense competitor with great body strength, who loved competition, but who was always a good sport." Richard Johnson, her senior-year coach, was quoted as saying, "Pat has scored a lot of points (28.1 per game) and been a great rebounder (averaged 14). We'll miss her. She was a great leader, a hard worker who never missed a practice or a game. She was always the first to arrive and the last to leave." In her senior year Pat was also named most popular girl by the student body and "Basketball Sweetheart of the Season."

Fifteen years after graduation, Pat was still popular at Cheatham County High. In January 1985, to honor her achievements as a basketball player and coach, and particularly to honor her as the coach of the 1984 women's gold medal Olympic team, the gym at her old school was named the "Pat Head Summitt Gymnasium." The community also raised $10,000 for a scholarship fund to award $1,000 annually to a female basketball player from Cheatham County High School. Each year a basketball game between alumni and the current team is played (using old six-player rules) with proceeds going to the Pat Head Summitt scholarship fund. Pat participated in the first game in 1985.

A trophy case above the corridor in the Pat Head Summitt Gymnasium displays memorabilia of Pat's basketball career. It includes photographs of her as a player at the elementary, high school, and college levels, and as a coach of the Lady Vols and the Olympic team. Her high school jersey, Number 55, is also displayed along with an oil painting of the most famous graduate of Cheatham County High School. Even Pat's father is pleased with the "Pat Head Summitt Gymnasium."

When Pat Head entered the University of Tennessee at Martin (UTM) in the fall of 1970, Richard Nixon was president, Spiro Agnew was vice president, and the Vietnam War was raging. On March 26 of that same year, exactly 50 years after the 19th Amendment went into effect, the National Organization for Women (NOW) sponsored a Women's Strike for Equality. The strike, held in several major cities across the United States, focused on employment and educational equality and marked a new beginning for women's liberation efforts. The tone of the times is evident from a quote by Jane Pollock, head of the Boston chapter of NOW. Noting the weather on the day of the strike, Pollock said, "God has blessed us in the Movement with a beautiful day—hasn't She."

By 1974, the year Pat finished college, the Vietnam War had ended, Nixon and Agnew had resigned in disgrace, and efforts by people involved in the women's liberation movement had resulted in, among other things, the passage of federal legislation, Title IX of the Education Amendments to the Civil Rights Act, guaranteeing women equal educational opportunities in all fields, including athletics. But because the legislation, passed in 1972, did not mandate compliance until 1976, Pat and her teammates at UTM realized none of the benefits during their collegiate playing days.

Pat Head had chosen to attend UTM because it was one of the few schools that had an intercollegiate basketball program for women. The program had only been in existence since 1969.

Nadine Gearin, Pat's coach throughout her college career, had been assigned the position almost by default, since she was the only member of the women's physical education staff who had played basketball in high school. There were virtually no college basketball teams in those days, so it was nearly impossible to find a woman who had played beyond the high school level. Gearin coached volleyball and tennis at UTM in addition to teaching physical education. As did most women coaches of the era, Gearin spent her own money to transport her team to other cities for games.

The climax of Pat's freshman season at Martin was the first intercollegiate state basketball tournament, sponsored by the Tennessee Women's Sports Federation. Gearin's squad, led by 5-10 forward Pat Head, won.

A photograph of that victorious UTM women's basketball team reveals a solemn Pat Head wearing a too-large jersey with a slightly askew Number 22. Team members had been responsible for making their own numbers and sewing them on their uniforms. Apparently, some of the members were not particularly adept with a needle and thread. By Pat's second season, UTM had purchased real uniforms, and Pat can be seen in sophomore-year photos wearing her favorite Number 55.

In 1971, the Association for Intercollegiate Athletics for Women (AIAW) was established. In 1972, the organization sponsored a national basketball championship at Illinois State University in Normal. The UTM team, led by its outstanding forward, Pat Head, won at the district, state, and regional levels to qualify as one of the 16 teams competing in the nationals. They won their opening game against Long Beach State, but lost to the eventual fourth-place winner, Mississippi University for Women. The champion of the inaugural AIAW event was Immaculata College, a small Catholic women's college in Pennsylvania, which also won in 1973 and 1974.

The national exposure was great for Pat's basketball career. As a result, she was invited to try out for the World University Games and made the United States team that competed in Moscow in 1973. That experience launched Pat on the road to international fame as a player and then as a coach.

In Pat's junior year, her team posted a 22-3 record, but lost at the state level to UTK by a score of 59-57. In Pat's senior year, during the seventh game of the season she suffered a severe knee injury. Everybody, including Pat, thought her basketball career was over. Indeed, she was not able to rejoin her college team. But during the next 2 years, while coaching and working on her master's degree in physical education at the University of Tennessee at Knoxville, Pat rehabilitated her knee and eventually played on the 1976 United States women's Olympic squad.

Despite her aborted senior season, Pat's college career had been a great one. She had established several UTM records that as of this writing have yet to be broken: most career points—1,405; most career free throws—361; most points in season—530 in 1971-72; and most free throws in a season—132 in 1971-72.

Nadine Gearin, no longer in athletics but still teaching physical education at Martin, says of Pat, "She's the best athlete we've ever had here, man or woman. She was a great, great player."

Bettye Giles, UTM athletic director, remembers the first time she ever saw Pat. The tall, sturdy freshman strode into her office in September of 1970 and asked, "When does basketball start?"

When Giles explained that basketball didn't start until volleyball season was over, Pat was unable to hide her frustration. Bettye realized immediately that although Pat had probably never played volleyball, she would make an excellent addition to the Martin team. With this in mind, she said to Pat, "Volleyball is an excellent conditioner for basketball. Why don't you try out for that team, then if you make it, you'll be in great shape when basketball season begins." Bettye convinced Pat of the merits of volleyball, and Summitt played that sport as well as basketball during her 4 years as an undergraduate. Nadine Gearin, who coached both sports, was delighted to have the 5-10 freshman on both squads and recalls that Pat was a "pretty good" volleyball player. "But," she added, "she never really liked the game."

For her first 2 years, Pat played ball in the only gym on campus. The facility accommodated the physical education programs, an intramural program, the varsity men's basketball team, the women's varsity volleyball team, and the fledgling women's basketball program. No wonder it was almost impossible to find practice time. Sometimes Pat's team didn't get the gym until 11:00 at night.

Although Pat played only 2 years in the old gym (a new facility was built in 1972) she will never forget the place. A part of it will always be with her—literally. In one of the most unusual gifts ever presented, Pat Head Summitt was given one of the basketball goals, including the backboard and supports, from the old gym where she had played as a college freshman and sophomore. In making the presentation at halftime of one of UTM's football games, then Chancellor Larry McGehee said, "Now, Pat, you will always have the goal where you scored your first two collegiate points."

Bettye Giles recalls the occasion this way: "I was on the committee to select a gift for Pat in honor of her participation as a player in the 1976 Olympics, but when the committee couldn't agree what to present, the chancellor announced he would make the decision." Giles pauses to laugh. "Can you imagine our amazement when we found out what it was? I know Pat was disappointed."

Why would Pat be disappointed with such an extraordinary gift? Says Giles, "Placed on the football field, covered by a huge tarp, the thing was so big, it looked like a car."

Diplomat that she is, Pat never complained.

Getting "the thing" home was a problem. Nadine Gearin kept it in the yard at her house for a long time. Finally, Pat drove her dad's truck over to Martin and brought the gigantic remembrance back to her folk's place in Henrietta. It remains there today.

In some ways Pat Summitt was in college during the best years of women's sports. Colleges were just beginning to provide sports opportunities for women, yet competition was not yet so all-consuming that they couldn't enjoy other aspects of college life. Pat was an active member of Chi Omega and played for her sorority on various intramural teams.

Nor did Pat's social life suffer because of her athletic schedule. She had a wide circle of friends who loved to party, and Pat learned to drink beer with the best of them. Then as now, she loved to drive fast, and on more than one occasion, she talked herself out of speeding tickets. Despite her wild side, Pat was popular with faculty and students. "When Pat was at Martin, she knew everybody and everybody knew her," said Bettye Giles. "Not just on campus, but in town, and everybody loved her." Giles explained that, "Even now, when Pat comes back, it's hard to get to see her 'cause so many folks ask her to dinner, or just to come by for coffee; she's either visiting or on the phone the whole time she's here."

Pat is at Martin often. She has received all the awards her alma mater has to offer, including, along with Gearin and Giles, induction into the UTM Sports Hall of Fame, and, along with Governor Ned McWherter, the Outstanding Alumni award.

Pat keeps up with the current UTM teams, and sends personal notes to players when they break her records. The young woman who has already received a few such notes and may receive several more is 6-4-1/2 junior center Mary Kate Long. Long, an English major, wrote a paper entitled "Pat Head Summitt—A Living Legend" for a folklore course in the spring of 1988. The final paragraph reads, "Pat does embody the qualities we Americans look for in our heroes: determination, a willingness to work hard, a God-given talent, and a giving personality that finds satisfaction in using one's talents to make others happy! . . . Her example is a noble one for anyone to follow—especially for an athlete. I have greatly enjoyed getting to know more of Pat Head Summitt through my research of the folklore surrounding her life here at this university. I must say now more than ever I am very proud to be a Lady Pacer."

CHAPTER FIVE

Turning Points

When Pat injured her knee in her senior year at UTM, she decided to stay involved in the game of basketball by becoming a coach. So she applied for a graduate assistantship at UTK and was awarded the grant for the school year beginning in the fall of 1974. That was the year Nixon's successor, Gerald Ford, signed into law Title IX, the legislation that mandated equal opportunity for females in athletics. It was also the year that a 22-year-old grad student named Pat Head began her legacy as one of the finest coaches in the game of women's basketball.

After spending the first month at UTK settling into the routine of attending and teaching classes, Pat began her "real" job of coaching the Tennessee women's basketball team. Tryouts for the team—the Volettes, as they were referred to then—were announced in a small column in the *Daily Beacon*, the student newspaper, in October of 1974. Sixty-five women reported to Alumni Gym at the appointed time. There they were met by Pat Head, a well-known basketball player from the University of Tennessee at Martin, who was about to begin her coaching career. Pat, by her own admission, was lacking in many of the finer points of basketball, but she was not lacking in her ability to condition players. On the second night of practice, after enduring the strenuous running drills of the rookie head coach, the squad had been reduced substantially, and as practices continued, Pat did not have to cut many players. The women selected themselves, so to speak, until 12 women emerged as the 1974-75 team.

Pat had inherited the position from Margaret Hutson, who had compiled in her four seasons at Tennessee a record of 71 wins and 17 losses. A good coach, Hutson was better known for her ability to "con" everybody (local businesses as well as university personnel) into providing things for her basketball team. For example, she convinced an ice company to donate an ice machine, pleaded with administrators to give her an old equipment closet in Alumni Gym, and transformed the room into a training facility complete with a taping table and ice.

A writer for the *Daily Beacon* once interviewed Coach Hutson and, in a front-page story, detailed the impoverished circumstances of the women's basketball team. Hutson was elated. Surely sympathetic readers, discovering that the Volettes had to sell doughnuts to support their team, would send large sums of money in response. But alas, the only response was from a local alumnus who wanted to sell Hutson a doughnut machine at a reduced price!

But with the passage of Title IX, Hutson knew that the sport of women's basketball was bound to evolve beyond her. She had never played the game herself, felt insecure in the position of coach, and did not want the pressure that would inevitably arrive. So she turned the program over to young Pat Head.

Pat's team consisted of 12 white women, all from Tennessee. The tallest player was 5-10 center/forward Gail Dobson, none of the players had athletic scholarships, and none had played five-player, full-court basketball.

The fact that the state of Tennessee was one of the last strongholds of six-player, split-court basketball for high school girls posed problems for Coach Head. In this system, girls played either offense or defense, and once they became college players it was often difficult to make the transition to the full-court, five-player game. It was particularly difficult for athletes who had been guards in high school to master the shooting skills required of college players.

Pat was also faced with the problem of ankle-taping. Hutson had been adept at this, but the rookie coach had never taped an ankle, and didn't believe it was necessary. Many of her athletes came around to her view of taping, and those who didn't learned to rely on Teresa Loveday, the student manager.

Only 50 spectators, "including custodians," says Pat, came to see her first game, between UTK and then-powerhouse Mercer University. Just before the game began, the captain, Diane Brady, asked Pat if she was nervous. Pat's immediate response was "no."

Unconvinced, Brady then asked the head coach, "Why is your neck so red?" Indeed, Pat's neck flushes when she is extremely nervous. She now remembers that the jitters she felt before that first college game rank among the worst she has ever suffered. "I was just like a duck—cool and calm on top, but paddling like crazy underneath," she says.

Tennessee lost that game, 84-83. Afterward, when Pat was discussing the game with her brother, Tommy, she was unable to tell him what kind of defense the Mercer coach had used against Tennessee. ''I could only see the Tennessee team,'' she says. "It never occurred to me to look at Mercer's defense.''

February 4, 1975, marked a turning point for Tennessee women's basketball; it finally became a spectator sport. Tennessee Tech came to Knoxville with a 10-1 record, having lost only to Delta State, the defending national champions, and Tennessee had also suffered only one loss, to Tech in their first meeting. For the first time ever, reporters hounded the coordinator of women's athletics for tickets, and were shocked to learn there were no tickets; the game was free.

Tom Siler, then sports editor of the *Knoxville News-Sentinel*, was one of those who took advantage of the free game and attended with his wife. This is his account of the contest:

Speaking of girls, Nancy and I went over the other night to see the Tennessee coeds play Tennessee Tech. We were impressed. They lost by two, but that's beside the point. They play under the 30-second clock. The girls really move the ball, knock each other around (accidentally, of course) and play with tremendous intensity. The UT pep band was there along with 700 or so yelling fans. Pat Head's gals have an excellent fast break, but in this particular game, Tech had the height, so the Vols got the quick release only a few times. The game was lively and exciting, well officiated, too. And the two coaches sat on the bench, and that was a pleasant innovation, too.

Siler said there were 700 in attendance; the *Daily Beacon* estimated the crowd at 2,000, and Pat recalls "a full house," which would make it around 3,000. At any rate, there were spectators, which in itself was unusual for a women's game.

Pat Head survived that first season with a respectable 16 wins and 8 losses. The next year, Pat was asked to name her Number 1 priority for the Lady Vols. Her response had nothing to do with winning games or championships. Instead, she said she would like to have her team play before a sellout crowd in Stokely Athletics Center.

By 1976 the women's team had made it into 12,700-seat Stokely Athletics Center, and they played there until 1987. During this 11-year span, Summitt's largest crowd was estimated to be 10,000 against LSU in 1979. By 1987 Summitt had reached other goals, including two Olympic medals and a national championship, but her original dream was still unfulfilled.

When plans for a new 25,000-scat basketball facility were announced in 1981, there had been some discussion about whether the Lady Vols should move there or continue to play in Stokely. It was then that Coach Summitt decided that playing before a full-house in a 25,000-seat arena would be a greater achievement than playing before 12,700 in the soon-to-be-outdated Stokely.

Pat's first chance to fill the house and not only fulfill her own vision but also break the national attendance record for women's basketball came on December 9, 1987, when Tennessee played Texas. The game was a natural sellout. Tennessee, the defending national champion, was ranked Number 1 and Texas Number 2 at the time of the contest. Moreover, there was a heated rivalry between the two schools. The previous year the teams had met twice: Tennessee defeated Texas in Austin, and Texas was victorious in the Orange Bowl Classic in Florida. If such conditions had existed for a men's game, Tennessee might have started building a 50,000-seat arena.

Just to be sure of a sellout, the athletic department instigated an intensive marketing campaign, and Wendy's, the hamburger chain, purchased 20,000 tickets to distribute free of charge with a food purchase. In fact, Wendy's distributed 80,000 tickets since its research indicated that only one in four ticket-holders actually attend. But Dr. Boling, president of the university, was dubious about Wendy's marketing research figures. He called Joan Cronan, women's athletic director, to ask about contingency plans if 80,000 fans appeared for seats in a facility with a capacity of approximately 25,000.

As it turned out, Dr. Boling's fears were well-founded. There were several hundred more fans than seats, and the contingency plan was implemented: Wendy's tickets would be honored at the next Lady Vol home game. This solution angered many fans, especially the family whose father was admitted but whose mother and children, several yards behind, were locked out. Fortunately, one of the ushers was able to retrieve the unhappy father, who had the car keys. Undoubtedly, the Lady Vols did not endear themselves to this particular group.

Number 4 Dawn Marsh

Basketball purists were also upset. John Adams, sports editor of the *Knoxville News-Sentinel*, wrote a satirical column on the subject:

When you arrive at the Thompson-Boling Arena, you notice the parking lot is full of of buses. You also notice every bus driver is wearing a ski mask.

After each busload is escorted into the arena, the gunmen disappear. An usher leads you to your seat and hands you an envelope. The note inside is from the Lady Vols: "Thanks for making us No. 1."

"How can they count this as a record?" you ask the usher. "I didn't pay for the ticket. I was brought to the game at gunpoint." "As long as you came, it doesn't matter," the usher says. "We checked with the NCAA."

The turnstile count of spectators at the game was 24,563, and two representatives of the *Guinness Book of World Records* were present to attest that a new attendance record for women's basketball had, in fact, been established. Yet there was debate over which record was broken. According to the NCAA , the record of 15,514 was established between Texas and Louisiana Tech. The record recognized by Guinness was 22,157, the number of spectators who attended the Iowa–Ohio State game on February 3, 1985.

The reason for the discrepancy was that Carver-Hawkeye Arena, site of the Iowa–Ohio State game, had a seating capacity of 15,400; because of this, the official paid attendance was reported as 14,821. Had the actual number of 22,157 been reported, Iowa officials would have been in trouble with fire marshals. (Incidentally, a fast-food chain promotion, similar to the one at Tennessee, was primarily responsible for the large crowd at Iowa.) Although the number of fans who attended the Iowa–Ohio State game is debatable, there is no doubt a record was set in Iowa. For the first time in history, attendance at a sporting event was actually deflated.

The basketball game in Knoxville was a huge disappointment for Tennessee fans. The Tennessee players appeared satisfied that their work was over once the attendance goal was reached, and they were not able to demonstrate their basketball skills to the huge throng. Texas, of course, had something to do with that. It was one of those rare moments in sport when a team performs almost to perfection. As one long-time basketball fan was heard to remark, "Those Lady Longhorns played the best man-to-man defense of any team, male or female, that I have ever seen."

The Texas defense was not the only problem for the Lady Vols. Clarissa Davis, the 6-1 junior, who was the 1986-87 Naismith Player of the Year, scored 45 points, mostly from a 10-foot turnaround jumper, and was all over the court with her defensive play. She had one of those games that is the dream of every athlete, but rarely happens.

So Summitt reached the summit in basketball attendance goals, but was devastated by the 19-point rout (97-78.) However, the Lady Vols had often lost to teams early in the year and come back to beat those same teams in postseason play. Lady Vol supporters, coaches, and players assured themselves that the team was simply having a slow start.

Two days after the Texas loss, the Tennessee team flew to the west coast for games against UCLA and Oregon State, two unranked teams. Players were disappointed about not getting to play Long Beach State (ranked 4th at the time) and Southern California (ranked 13th), but Coach Summitt explained that there had been a scheduling problem with the two ranked California teams, so she decided to schedule the Lady Bruins and the Lady Beavers instead.

Before the UCLA game, the team huddled in the locker room for their traditional recitation of the Lord's Prayer. For Lisa Webb, an ardent church-goer; student assistant Shelley Sexton, a former member of the Christian Athletes in Action team; and some of the other players, this ritual had specific religious meaning. For others, it was a soothing, predictable ceremony that focused their attention, provided a sense of tradition, and reminded them that more was going on than just a basketball game.

The game against UCLA was not easy. The Lady Vols led by only 38-35 at intermission. In the second half, Tennessee came to life. Dawn Marsh handed off seven assists, and Sheila Frost, who had been Tennessee's only bright spot against Texas with 21 points, continued her exceptional shooting, dropping in 20 points for a final score of 89-63.

Perhaps this year, junior center Sheila Frost would shine again. When Frost was still in high school, Summitt had made 16 trips to Pulaski, Tennessee, to watch the 6-4 center play. That was before the NCAA imposed restrictions on the number of times coaches could observe recruits' games, and Frost holds the record for the number of Summitt visits. But Pat was willing to make the 5-hour drive from Knoxville because Sheila was good—very good—and was being recruited by every major school in the country. Some schools sent representatives to every one of Sheila's games. Fortunately for the Lady Vols, Coach Summitt managed to sign this outstanding prospect, and her rookie season was outstanding.

But Frost had been hot and cold her sophomore year, scoring in double figures in 20 games but scoring less than six points in another 9 games. Her inconsistency had begun to bother her teammates, who would occasionally show their frustration by yelling "Concentrate! Don't miss the easy ones! Come *on*, Sheila!"

With teammates and coaches constantly riding her, Sheila felt pressured, perhaps more so than anyone else on the team. Sheila was the only "big girl" on the floor (with the exception of 6-2 Pearl Moore, who was still a freshman), and she felt it was her job to rebound, clean up the shots that others missed, block shots, and contribute significantly on offense.

But her family called her PeeWee for a reason—she didn't *feel* like she was 6-4, and she rarely acted like it on the court. "If the other team really wants the ball that much," her actions sometimes seemed to say, "they can have it." Her career objective was to become a social worker—to help people, not push them around, as was a center's job in basketball. This year, however, she was looking strong and confident. Maybe the team *could* depend on its big center after all.

Following the UCLA victory, the Lady Vols were treated to a day in Disneyland before flying on to Corvallis, Oregon. The Disneyland break worked wonders for the Tennessee team. They were terrific against Oregon State University, scoring 91 points and limiting Oregon State to 56. Sheila Frost continued her shooting spree, shooting nine of nine from the field; Bridgette Gordon also played exceptionally well.

The victory was just what Tennessee needed. After being humiliated by Texas and playing poorly against UCLA, the Lady Vols had finally played up to their potential.

They arrived in Knoxville on December 19—Sheila Frost's birthday—just in time for the game with Eastern Kentucky University. It was an obvious mismatch, with Tennessee winning 115-40. The 75-point defeat was the biggest loss ever for EKU. For the Lady Vols it was the second biggest victory margin; they had blown away Hawaii Pacific in the 1985-86 season by a 92-point decision. They had also beaten Marshall University by 75 points in the 1976-77 season.

From the winning team's perspective, massacres are helpful in that they provide an opportunity for nonstarters to play a great deal. Against EKU, for example, Pearl Moore and Kris Durham played 19 and 21 minutes, respectively. Moore played extremely well, scoring 18 points, grabbing seven rebounds, and blocking four shots. Not too many people were there to enjoy the show, however: the attendance was 3,492—quite a contrast to the record-setting crowd of 24,563 who had attended the previous Lady Vol home game.

The final preholiday game was in Knoxville against Northern Illinois University. NIU's coach, Jane Albright, had served as Pat Summitt's graduate assistant from 1981 to 1983, and Albright's knowledge of the Tennessee system was apparent from her team's performance. But Tennessee still overpowered NIU 103-76. For the third game of the season, Tennessee went over the century mark, and Tonya Edwards had scored the 100th point in all three games.

Finally, on the night of December 20, the players were free to enjoy Christmas vacation. Regular students had been on vacation since December 10, and the women's basketball team was eager to join them. At this point, they had a record of seven wins and the one loss to Texas. For most teams this would have been a great start, but for the Lady Vols it was a disappointment. They had beaten mediocre teams by huge margins, but in their only real test, they had come up short.

CHAPTER SIX

Haunted by Texas

Nineteen eighty-seven may be remembered as the year of the scandal. Insider-trading on Wall Street disgraced that once-respected mecca of finance; the Iran-Contra affair shook the country; and sex scandals destroyed the careers of presidential hopeful Gary Hart and TV evangelists Jim Bakker and Jimmy Swaggart. In men's athletics, where scandals are common-place, 1987 was particularly devastating, with the NCAA's investigating several schools, including the football program at Tennessee. The final month of 1987 was more promising: Ronald Reagan and Mikhail Gorbachev signed a treaty eliminating intermediate-range nuclear missles.

The game of women's basketball can seem insignificant by comparison. But if you are a Lady Vol, basketball takes precedence regardless of what happens nationally or internationally. You go to classes, you study, you graduate, you might even read the newspaper or, like Bridgette Gordon, major in political science, but the truth is, you breathe, eat, and sleep basketball. So does your coach.

So from the perspective of the Lady Volunteers, 1987 had been a magnificent year. They had won the NCAA national championship and had established themselves as the best women's college team in the United States. Now, in 1988, Coach Summitt and her team looked forward to the challenge of staying on top.

In the first January game, the Lady Vols defeated the University of Illinois at Champaign, 93-59. Kris Durham made a three-pointer when the team needed a lift, and in her 23 minutes of playing time scored 11 points. More important, Kris was confident and poised, and the team responded well to her leadership. Though just a freshman, Kris was beginning to display the qualities Summitt expected of her point guards: intelligence, mental toughness, resilience. She hadn't taken the starting position from Dawn Marsh, but Summitt didn't need her to.

After their Sunday game with Illinois, the team returned to Knoxville for a Tuesday game with Northwestern, which they won, 78-65. Then the race for the Southeastern Conference championship began with Tennessee's first league game, against Auburn, January 9.

Due to a snowstorm, the university, as well as the rest of Knoxville and much of the Southeast, had been shut down on Thursday and Friday, and there was some question whether Auburn would be able to make the Saturday trip. Fortunately, the weather cleared enough for the team bus to travel from Auburn, Alabama, to Knoxville.

Tennessee had lost to Auburn twice the previous season, but had beaten them soundly in Knoxville (77-61) in the Mideast regional, which had sent the Lady Vols to the Final Four and the eventual national championship. This season they both had lost to top-ranked teams: Tennessee to Texas and Auburn to Iowa. These defeats had shaken up the national rankings; Tennessee was now ranked fourth and Auburn second. The winner would be a decided favorite to win the Southeastern Conference championship.

The game was closely contested for the entire 40 minutes. But Auburn guard Ruthie Bolton intercepted a pass in the closing seconds and raced the length of the court for an uncontested two points, sealing their 71-68 victory.

The disappointing loss to Auburn coupled with the Texas defeat had the potential to prove devastating for the Lady Vols. These were the sort of losses that could lead to low morale, team dissension, and ultimately more failure. Could team members still console themselves that early-season losses led to later-season victories? Or was losing the big games beginning to be a pattern? The defending champs were worried.

Following the Auburn defeat on Saturday, the Lady Vols practiced on Sunday and then left by bus on Monday for a game against Georgia Tech in Atlanta. Summitt, too, was concerned that her team might not perform well. But as the cheer goes, the Lady Vols wrecked Tech, 96-79.

Number 35 Melissa McCray vs. Auburn

In her best game of the young season, Tonya Edwards was outstanding. She scored a career-high 23 points, making 10 of 13 field goal attempts. She also had five rebounds, five steals, and four assists. Sheila Frost had another fine game, especially defensively. Georgia Tech's leading scorer, 6-7 center Delores Bootz, had been averaging 23 points, and Frost held her to only 8. A satisfying victory for Tennessee.

The game was particularly satisfying for Tonya Edwards. The youngest of six children (all having names beginning with "T,") Tonya was used to having to prove herself, but living up to Pat's expectations was tough. It was also tough to share the court with Bridgette Gordon. Not that Bridgette wasn't cordial, and even helpful, but Gordon had a way of so dominating the floor that even her teammates could be intimidated. Between Pat's yelling and Gordon's larger-than-life example, Tonya wasn't sure just where she fit in with this team. But against Georgia Tech, Tonya had felt comfortable, competent, in charge. Her mother and brother Terry, who frequently came down from Michigan to watch her play, would be proud.

There wasn't time to celebrate. After the game, the Lady Vols stopped for a snack, then boarded the bus for the 3-1/2-hour trip home. They arrived in Knoxville at 2:00 a.m., and since every team member had Tuesday classes, it was going to be a short night.

When the team reported for their regular practice at 12:30 p.m. on Tuesday, the coaches were assured that everybody had made it to class. There was no assurance, however, that every Lady Vol had stayed awake for the lectures. In fact, they were barely awake as Coach Summitt began the workout. Their fatigue was understandable when one considers their schedule: Saturday—loss to Auburn in Knoxville; Sunday—rigorous practice; Monday—victory over Georgia Tech in Atlanta (3-1/2-hour bus trip each way); Tuesday—morning classes and a 12:30 practice.

Coach Summitt was not sympathetic. When the team did not execute a 1-3-1 zone according to Pat's specification, she said in disgust, "Let's quit this. If you can't play zone, we'll spend 40 minutes playing man-to-man, which you don't do very well either." The practice ended with running drills, which had taken on a new dimension since the Texas defeat. Players who had failed to box-out on rebounds during the previous game were required to run a "change drill" for each infraction. The drill required players to sprint the length of the court for a timed period of 97 seconds. When the coach yelled "change," the runner changed directions. Ninety-seven seconds was the number of points Texas had scored against Tennessee earlier in the season. On this day, Dawn Marsh and Pearl Moore had to run two such drills. Their teammates shouted encouragement as they ran.

The Texas loss was a sore spot among players and coaches alike. Pat and her assistants had been humiliated, and feared further humiliation in the future if the team did not improve. The players were afraid, too, but the way they saw it, dwelling on the loss—not the loss itself—was what would hold them back.

In fact, in a preseason session with sport psychologist Tina Buckles, the team had signed a pact with the coaches addressing this very point. In addition to other points of conduct, the players and coaches had agreed not to dwell on defeat. The players had raised this issue because they felt unduly punished after losing games in previous years.

So when Coach Summitt ordered the running drills, there were a few sidelong glances among the players. They had already protested to Buckles that they didn't appreciate Summitt's mentioning the Texas defeat at virtually every practice. Nor did they appreciate the fact that Summitt had painted the score of the Texas game on a locker room wall. Buckles had consulted with the coach, who did not remove the score from the wall but did promise to refer to the Texas rout less frequently.

But as if determined not to let the ghost of Texas dampen their spirits, the players laughed and kidded with each other and the assistant coaches during postpractice stretching. When the team was dismissed, Dawn Marsh ran over to Mickie DeMoss, picked up the 100-pound assistant coach, threw her over her shoulder, and began running down the court. As Dawn ran and DeMoss kicked and screamed, Marsh yelled to her teammates, "This will be Pat's next addition to the change drill. We'll have to carry a coach." The team laughed uproariously as Dawn continued to run with protesting Mickie.

Then someone said, "Thank God none of the coaches is too fat." Someone else added, "Except Holly." Practice ended on a happy note.

Holly Warlick is not fat. But she can take a joke, especially since she is at home on the UTK court, almost literally. A native of Knoxville, Frances Hollingsworth ("Holly") Warlick came to UTK as a student in 1976, and received one of Tennessee's first women's athletic scholarships. The award was for track, not basketball. Pat Summitt had not offered Holly a basketball scholarship, and she only made the team as a walk-on.

Besides being the first to have women's scholarships, that 1976-77 team was the first to play in Stokely Athletics Center, and the first to go to nationals, where they finished third. They lost to eventual winner and

Bridgette Gordon, Holly Warlick, Pat Summitt, Mickie DeMoss

defending champion Delta State, but enroute to the semifinal game soundly defeated a previous champion, Immaculata, 91-71. Says Holly, "That trip to nationals put Tennessee women's basketball on the map."

Holly competed in nationals in track that year, too, placing fourth in the 400-yard relay. But running track early in the morning, attending classes, going to basketball practice, then sprinting back to the track for more running workouts was a demanding schedule, and the 18-year-old knew she could not keep up the pace. After her freshman year, she decided to concentrate on basketball.

It was a happy choice for Lady Vol basketball fans. Holly had a glorious career, sharing the court with such greats as Cindy Brogdon (1977-79), Cindy Noble (1978-81), and Lea Henry (1979-83). Warlick was a three-time all-American while playing for Pat and the first player, male or female, to have her jersey (Number 22) retired. She still holds Tennessee records for most assists in a season (225) and most steals in a game (9).

Despite her success, Warlick remembers those early years as turbulent times. After the first week of practice the freshman said to herself, "This lady [Pat] is crazy." One of the crazier tactics, according to Holly, was

Pat's habit of having them run for 30-minute stretches without ever touching a basketball. Pat was only 25, Holly points out, and trying to prove herself, but most of the players thought her conditioning program was ridiculous.

Yet no one left the squad. ''We'd mimic Pat and fuss among ourselves about her all the time, but we never considered quitting.''

Holly also remembers receiving the brunt of Pat's anger. ''Pat yelled at me most of all. It became a joke. Before practice the rest of the team would kid, 'Well, guess this will be another Holly day.' '' Holly later realized that this was Summitt's way of helping Holly improve, because the freshman had never played five-player basketball before. Holly also realized that she responded to Pat's yelling by working harder, so the head coach kept up the pressure.

Holly still remembers one particular practice when she was a freshman, the morning after she and her teammates had had a late-night party. Somehow Coach Summitt had found out about it, and when the team members arrived at practice the next day, they knew something was up because trash cans had been placed at each of the four corners of the old Alumni Gym basketball court. No one asked about them because it was clear that the coach was not in the best of moods.

When practice started, they realized immediately the purpose of the cans. Anyone who has had to run strenuously after a night of imbibing will be able to relate to the condition of the Lady Vols that day. One by one, they hung their heads over the well-placed trash cans, vomited, then without a word from either coach or athlete, returned to the running drills. Except for the gags and heaves, there was complete silence during the entire 30-minute ordeal.

Like Dawn Marsh, Holly was a prankster, so the work-study grant that required her to work a few hours per week in the athletic department offered her an opportunity for fun. The university was just beginning to recruit athletes in those days, and athletic director Gloria Ray would often dispatch Holly to pick up the young athletes at the airport, loaning Holly her late-model Cadillac for the trips. ''Gloria never knew,'' confesses Holly, ''but I always told the recruits as soon as they got in that big ole car that this is what they gave me when I signed at Tennessee.''

After 4 years at UTK, Holly was drafted by the Nebraska Wranglers of the Women's Basketball League. ''I loved Omaha,'' says Holly. ''The people were great and it was wonderful to get paid for doing something I really enjoyed.'' Her salary was $22,000 plus incentives for winning; a contrast to the NBA average salary at the time—about $230,000. But the league went belly up the following year, and in the process Holly and her teammates never received their final two paychecks.

Next Holly earned a master's degree in athletic administration from Virginia Tech, then returned to Nebraska to serve as assistant coach at the University of Nebraska at Lincoln. When Pat offered her the assistant coach position at Tennessee, Holly yearned to return. Still, she had some hesitations. First, she feared people would think she had gotten the job only because of her former player-coach relationship, and that she would be construed as Pat's "yes person."

She had also interviewed with Pat 2 months before, and had been disappointed by Pat's reaction. "She was so cold and distant to me that I thought to myself that I would rather fight another winter in Nebraska than return to Knoxville." So when Pat made the offer, Holly talked to her about her concerns before accepting. Now Holly says, "It has worked out fine. Pat asks my opinion and although we don't always agree, we get along well, and the three of us—Pat, Mickie, and myself—are a great team. Pat is a worrier, Mickie is a semiworrier, and I'm an optimist. We respect each other and that makes all the difference."

Though Mickie DeMoss is the primary recruiter, Holly helps with that chore and assists with practice and game planning. Holly also makes all the travel arrangements and handles the money for away trips.

One of Holly's least favorite tasks is public speaking. But last year, when Mickie was scheduled to speak at the commencement for Clinton Junior High School, she asked Holly to fill in for her. Mickie was vacationing in Florida and wanted to stay a few extra days, so, as she says, "Momma didn't raise no fool," and she asked Holly to take on the task. "You'll only have to say a few words," Mickie promised.

Warlick agreed to pinch-hit and arrived at the appointed hour. When she got there she was astonished to find a packed auditorium and even more astonished when she asked, "Who's the speaker?" and was told, "You are." Holly had one thought: "I'm going to kill DeMoss."

Fortunately, Holly had done enough public speaking to be able to ad lib "a great motivational speech," she remembers. But on second thought, she adds, "It must not have been too great. They didn't invite me back this year."

Others still invite her to speak at various functions. Recently when someone called from the Sertoma Club, Holly was heard to respond to the caller, "You know, my fee for a luncheon talk is $200." After a pause for the caller's response, she said, "Okay, I'll settle for lunch."

Holly's mother and sister, who still live in Knoxville, continue to attend all the Lady Vols' home games, as they did when she was a player. They are great coaches, Holly notes. "They second-guess our every move. I

have to constantly justify our substitutions as well as other stategies."
Holly's one regret is that her father, who died when she was in high school,
did not live to see her play college ball.

About her relationship with the head coach, Holly says, "I owe Pat
a lot. She's like a second Mom to me. She certainly helped me to grow
up, but I also think Mickie and I help Pat. We lighten her up and show
her there's more to life than being so serious all the time about basketball."

CHAPTER SEVEN

Coaching Summitt Style

The Old Dominion game on January 14 was a rematch for the two teams who had met at the beginning of the season at the Communiplex Classic in Cincinnati. Tennessee had won that game decisively, but under new coach, Wendy Larry, Old Dominion had been steadily improving. They came to Knoxville with a four-game winning streak that included a victory over highly regarded Western Kentucky.

In the rematch with the Lady Vols, the Lady Monarchs' improvement was evident, and the Lady Vols again played poorly. They seemed tired, which was understandable, given their January schedule. Summitt, however, made no mention of the schedule at halftime.

"Play a more up-tempo game!" she implored them. She was particularly upset with the play of both Tonya Edwards and Kris Durham. Shouted Summitt at Edwards, "Tonya, you commit to the Tennessee tempo or you don't play." Her remarks to Durham were equally vehement. "Kris, if that's all the speed you've got, you might as well put on your warm-ups."

Apparently Summitt's motivational strategy for Tonya worked. Although she didn't start the second half, Tonya came off the bench and scored 11 points in a 4-minute span for a total of 15 points. Kris, however, had several turnovers and failed to record a point in 11 minutes of play.

When the final buzzer sounded and the scoreboard showed that Tennessee was victorious, 91-68, the Lady Vols filed into the locker room as if they had just lost a championship. Summitt huddled outside with her assistants. "I'm worried about this team," she said. "We seem to never get mentally prepared when we play at home. We think we can come out and automatically win."

The other coaches agreed. Mickie DeMoss added, "Pat, I think they are immature. They have too many distractions."

Summitt was in apparent agreement with DeMoss because the first thing she said to the team was, "You need to grow up. You have too many distractions." She added."You play like you did tonight and Vandy [Vanderbilt] will kick your behinds on Sunday." Pat congratulated Bridgette Gordon and Pearl Moore, but admonished Dawn to stick to the fundamentals. "Dawn," she said, "you can hotdog all over the European basketball league when you finish at Tennessee, but until that time you've got to keep it simple." Pat concluded by saying, "Enjoy your victory. Take tomorrow off and concentrate on your studies. Saturday's practice will be at 2:00 p.m." With that, the coaches departed. The tired, solemn defending national champions slowly began to shed their sweaty uniforms.

Pat trusts Mickie DeMoss. The diminutive former player knows basketball, knows people, and knows how to entice 17-year-olds to come play basketball at Tennessee. Though it is never in doubt who is in charge, when Mickie speaks, Pat listens.

During her playing days, little Mickie DeMoss was a point guard at Louisiana Tech, and she has the distinction of having played on Coach Sonja Hogg's first team there in 1973. Leon Barmore, the present Tech coach, began as Hogg's assistant in Mickie's senior season.

After graduating from Tech, Mickie served as a graduate assistant under Mary Lou Johns at Memphis State University, and when she completed her master's degree in physical education, DeMoss stayed on as a full-time assistant.

In 1979, DeMoss became the nation's youngest head coach at a Division I school when she accepted the position at the University of

Florida. Perhaps she was too young; in any case, she didn't get along with the administration and resigned in 1983 to accept a position as recruiting coordinator for Joe Ciampi at Auburn. During her 3-year Auburn tenure, DeMoss earned the reputation of being one of the finest recruiters in the country.

When Nancy Darsch, who had been the sole Tennessee assistant for 10 years, left to accept a head coaching position at Ohio State, Summitt needed an assistant as well as a full-time recruiter. DeMoss had the ideal credentials for recruiting, and she gladly accepted the offer. She had admired Summitt for years, and believed that her team often won with inferior talent simply because of Summitt's knowledge of the game. With the addition of quality black players, whom DeMoss felt confident in recruiting, DeMoss knew the Lady Vols would be even better. She was also eager to disprove a prevailing perception in basketball circles that Pat Summitt could not coach blacks.

Her first year at UTK, DeMoss recruited Tonya Edwards, the 5-10 forward from Flint, Michigan, who was later named Most Valuable Player in the 1987 Final Four. Carla McGhee, Pearl Moore, and Daedra Charles are other top black athletes DeMoss has signed to play for the Lady Vols.

Spending several nights per week on the phone with 17-year-olds can be a bore, DeMoss admits. But she considers the phone calls an essential ingredient of her success. "A good recruiter must feel comfortable with folks, and have the gift of gab, as we say in Louisiana. Of course, you also must be able to assess talent, know how to sell your program, and be persistent."

DeMoss says the travel demands of the job may preclude her from keeping her position after she has children, but for now, she wouldn't consider working anywhere else, even as a head coach. At the end of the 1987 season, she was offered the head coach position at Arizona State, but declined. "Pat is one of the best in the business, and the Tennessee program is one of the most competitive. Pat stands for class and integrity, and working for her is a challenge since she never lets you relax!"

That's not entirely true: During a road trip to Los Angeles last year, DeMoss took time off to appear on the game show "The Price is Right." She won several items, including a trip to New Zealand.

But whom did she take with her to New Zealand? Pat and her husband, R.B. And what did they do while they were there? Conducted a basketball clinic at the Australian Institute of Sport. No wonder DeMoss and Summitt get along so well.

DeMoss and Summitt were in cahoots again on January 17, 1988, when the Lady Vols played Vanderbilt University. Both shuddered to remember last year's defeat to Vanderbilt, 77-76. Summitt, who had grown up in the shadow of the prestigious Nashville university, had been particularly upset by the loss.

Pat's team was well aware of the importance of the Vanderbilt game to their coach. This was obvious when the Tennessee women took to the arena floor. From the opening tip, the spectators could tell Tennessee had come to avenge last year's defeat. In the first half, Vanderbilt was held to 10 field goals and 10 free throws, making the halftime score Tennessee—52, Vanderbilt—30. The 52 points were the highest the Lady Vols had scored in one half this season. As a fan remarked, "Our Tennessee team is back." Indeed, this was by far their best game of the season.

Bridgette Gordon had an exceptional game. Nevertheless, Summitt screamed at her star forward during a time-out, "Bridgette, get down the floor and defend against penetration!" When Bridgette lowered her eyes and did not respond, Pat yelled, "Bridgette, look at me, respond!" Bridgette's response was not apparent.

Summitt's directive to Bridgette Gordon was not a private one. The Tennessee women's basketball program has a unique public relations gimmick that provides up to a dozen people per game with an opportunity to witness the head coach in action. At all home games, guest coaches are invited to sit behind the bench and to accompany the team into the locker room for halftime and postgame talks. These guest coaches can be faculty members, financial contributors, Boost-Her workers, or corporate executives. Corporate executives are always invited, for instance, when a particular company promotes a Lady Vol game.

The presence of these influential members of the Knoxville community does not deter Coach Summitt from what many of the pseudocoaches perceive as abuse of her players. One guest coach during the Vanderbilt game, for example, looked at her husband when Summitt was shouting at Bridgette and whispered, "My feelings are hurt just listening to Pat."

Her husband responded, "I'm ready to cry, I feel so sorry for Bridgette."

Pat is seemingly oblivious to the negative impression she makes on some of the athletically naive guest coaches, many of whom have never had such an intimate sport experience. Pat is equally as passionate when shouting at her team at a practice session as she is during a game with the "movers and shakers" of Knoxville and UTK sitting directly behind her.

But in this case, her strategy with Bridgette seemed to work. When Bridgette returned to the floor, she played with incredible intensity, hustling downcourt on defense and popping in a total of 26 points.

Sheila Frost also had an exceptional game, with a career-high 36 points, many of them with the aid of Dawn Marsh's 12 assists. The final score was 104-67, with Tonya Edwards, for the fourth time this season, scoring the two points that sent Tennessee over the century mark. The air in the Lady Vol dressing room was as festive as a New Year's Eve party at midnight. At last, Tennessee had played well and won. Even Coach Summitt smiled.

During Tuesday's practice, Pearl Moore and Kris Durham appeared dejected. Neither of the freshmen had played well in recent games, and the head coach had been extremely critical, particularly of Kris. Summitt continued to demand better defense from the point guard during practice, and from Pat's perspective, Kris was not responding well to the demands. When Kris appeared indifferent as the head coach was giving instructions about the upcoming South Carolina trip, Pat said to her, "Kris, do you want to go?" When Kris nodded, Summitt responded, "You don't act like it. Show a little enthusiasm."

When Pearl Moore mentioned that she would, because of a class, have to hurry to make the 4:45 departure time, Pat looked at her and said, "Pearl, I don't want to hear any complaining; you're lucky to get to go."

Summitt went on to explain that the main reason she was taking Pearl was because without her the Lady Vols might not have enough athletes to play against South Carolina. Sheila Frost, Bridgette Gordon, and Tonya Edwards were staying behind to attend Tuesday night classes, and would then fly to Columbia on Wednesday morning and return by bus with the team after the Wednesday evening game. Summitt was concerned that the flight might be canceled because of poor weather conditions, and Kathy Spinks, who had already missed the Old Dominion and Vanderbilt games due to a concussion she had suffered in practice, was still not able to play. With those four potentially missing, the squad was reduced to six players. Pearl was one of the six.

As it turned out, Summitt's concern about having enough players was unfounded. By the time the team arrived at Carolina Coliseum, there were nine healthy Lady Vols (Kathy Spinks did not make the trip) ready to don their orange away-game uniforms for the game against the underdog Lady Gamecocks.

In the first half Karen Middleton, South Carolina's outstanding freshman guard, hit five of six 3-pointers, and South Carolina led by 12 points at halftime. In the second half, the Lady Vols recovered their composure and pulled out an 85-80 victory.

Although displeased with her team's offensive rebounding, Coach Summitt was happy with their overall effort. The Lady Vols had overcome a 12-point halftime deficit to win by 5. "I'm proud of our team for winning under such pressure," she told them. Bridgette Gordon, Sheila Frost, and Lisa Webb had played well. Only Pearl Moore had played poorly, making one foul and several defensive mistakes in 2 minutes before being yanked out by Summitt.

The team arrived home at 2:00 a.m. and were given Thursday off. Practice resumed on Friday with a relatively subdued Coach Summitt. Pat is often subdued at the postgame practice sessions, talking objectively about team and individual strengths and weaknesses. Players and coaches sit in a circle in the middle of the gym floor, and the head coach makes her observations while asking individual players and coaches whether they agree with her assessments and what suggestions they have. During these sessions they appear to be colleagues, with everyone contributing ideas.

As the discussion came to a close, Pat announced that practice would be short today so that everyone would have a chance to review the South Carolina game films. Mickie generally has the responsibility of analyzing films with the team. This takes place in the Lady Vol locker room, and is again more of a collegial than a coach/athlete relationship. Players are encouraged to comment, and they often make insightful observations regarding their own play as well as the play of their teammates and opponents. Mickie acknowledges those insights by saying such things as "That's right, I hadn't seen that until you mentioned it."

The game against Alabama happened to be Pearl Moore's turn to have her picture on the cover of the program and to be the featured player of the game. Every Lady Vol is so honored each season, and perhaps being a cover girl inspired Pearl to a great performance. Whatever the reason, Moore came off the bench and played a total of 14 minutes, scoring 14 points, with eight rebounds and two blocked shots. Pearl had become a crowd pleaser, and when she left the game in the final minute, the 7,340 fans gave her a rousing cheer. Pearl smiled. Coach Summitt didn't smile, but she did pat the freshman on the back and say those wonderful words, "Good job, Pearl."

Number 4 Dawn Marsh vs. Alabama

For the first time in several outings, Tonya Edwards also played well. The offensive game was balanced, with Tonya, Bridgette, Sheila, and Lisa all in double figures.

There was one scary incident. Kathy Spinks, playing for the first time since her concussion, received another blow to the head, fell to the court, and lay still. After about 5 minutes, she was able to walk to the dressing room where the team doctor examined her and reported that Kathy had apparently not been seriously injured. The fans breathed a sigh of relief.

Coach Summitt was uncharacteristically complimentary to her team, and even singled out Tonya and Pearl, two players of late in the Summitt doghouse, for a Summitt smile and pat on the back. To the entire team, she said, "Good game. Enjoy your victory."

Then she outlined the schedule for the coming week. "We'll practice tomorrow [Sunday] at 2:30. This should give Lisa Webb plenty of time to go to church. There will be no practice Monday." The team cheered.

Seated behind the players, the guest coaches grinned. From the looks of this one postgame team meeting, they were undoubtedly impressed with Coach Summitt's calm demeanor and her positive-reinforcement coaching style. They probably attributed the defending national champions' success to their mild-mannered and supportive coach. Appearances can be deceiving!

CHAPTER EIGHT

A Bench Warmer's Lesson

Many great coaches have never played the sport they coached. But most of the time, a coach's experiences as a player not only teach her about the game itself, but give her essential insights into how it feels to play the game, which enables her to empathize with her players. In Pat Head Summitt's case, her playing experiences also taught her what it feels like to sit on the bench.

Pat Head Summitt's international career began in 1973, after her junior year in college, when she played in the World University Games in Moscow. Her selection as a member of the American team was a case of being in the right place at the right time.

Pat's 1972 UTM team had qualified for regionals, which were held in Boone, North Carolina. Patsy Neal, one of the best known women basketball players in the country (AAU all-American in 1959, 1960, and 1965), was in the stands that weekend, and, impressed with Pat's play, she persuaded the United States selection committee to invite the college junior to try out for the World University Games team. Based on Neal's recommendation, Summitt attended tryouts in Iowa and then Massachusetts, and she and 11 others were eventually selected to represent the United States at the World University Games. In spite of a 51-point defeat by the Soviet Union in the finals, the American team brought home a silver medal.

Jill Upton served as head coach of that team, with Billie Moore as the assistant. Upton was the head coach at Mississippi University for Women, one of the powers in women's basketball in the early seventies. Moore was coaching at California State University at Fullerton, and would later move to UCLA.

By her own admission, Pat was not a natural athlete, but she made up for the lack of natural ability through hard work, hustle, and exceptional stamina—attributes loved by all coaches. Players also admire these qualities, and Pat's teammates elected her co-captain of her first international team.

The Moscow trip established a professional relationship between Billie Moore and Pat Summitt that has grown through the years. Pat identifies Billie as one of the most "significant others" in her basketball life. She credits the Lady Bruin coach with teaching her the values of discipline and commitment in addition to practical knowledge about basketball techniques and strategies. When Pat has a basketball crisis, she still consults Moore. For instance, when Summitt was criticized in a 1978 *Sports Illustrated* article for accepting basketball players to UTK who were transferring from other schools, Pat called Moore for advice. Summitt also contacted the Lady Bruin coach when there was criticism over her selection of players to the 1984 Olympic team.

Membership on the World University Games team of 1973 had other rewards for Pat Summitt. As a result of the Moscow trip, Pat was selected as a member of the national team that in 1975 toured Taiwan, participated in the women's world championships in Cali, Columbia, and won the gold medal at the Pan American Games in Mexico City. Cathy Rush, the heralded mentor at Immaculata College, coached the U.S. team. Her assistant was Billie Moore.

Summitt's experience as a member of the 1975 American squad had a lasting influence on her coaching philosophy. Suddenly, Pat Summitt was a reserve. Having been a starter (and usually the star), this was a shock—especially since, as Pat recalls, her number was not called until her team had a 25-point advantage.

Having been a bench warmer, Summitt now possesses empathy for players who serve in reserve roles. According to her critics, she overcompensates, substituting too freely. Running players in and out of games as often as Pat does can not only disrupt the rhythm of the game, but prevent athletes from establishing their game tempo. Pat argues that frequent substitutions diffuse the star system and help her keep recruiting promises. But she also readily admits that she empties her bench as much as possible because she knows how much it means for the "scrubs" to get into the game.

Despite her reserve status, Pat was selected as a member of the 1976 United States Olympic team. Others chosen for the inaugural Olympic women's basketball squad included Nancy Lieberman, then a high school senior and the youngest member of the team; Lucia (Lucy) Harris, the great 6-3 center from Delta State University, who scored the first two points in women's Olympic competition; Ann Meyers, UCLA; Nancy Dunkle, California State at Fullerton; Juliene Simpson, John F. Kennedy College in Nebraska; Cindy Brogdon, Mercer University in Georgia; and Patricia Roberts, Emporia College in Kansas. Billie Moore was head coach. Her assistant, Sue Gunter, is a native of Mississippi who currently coaches at Louisiana State University.

After suffering a devastating first loss to underdog Japan, the United States had only one other defeat, a 112-77 loss to Russia, and finished with a silver medal. The Soviets, led by their outstanding 7-2 center, Iuliana Semonova, were the gold medalists. The first Olympics for women's basketball had been a huge success. The games also demonstrated that basketball programs for girls and women in the United States were producing players to be reckoned with at the international level.

At 24, Pat was the oldest player on the U.S. squad. She had already served 2 years as the head coach of the Lady Vols. Though she only played sparingly in the Olympic games, she was recognized for her leadership qualities by serving as co-captain of the team. As is the case with many amateur athletes, the Olympics brought to a close her competitive playing days.

But her coaching career was beginning to blossom. Having played with Summitt in Montreal, Trish Roberts and Cindy Brogdon both subsequently transferred to UTK to complete their undergraduate educations. With the help of Roberts, UTK placed third in the 1977 national championships, and with the help of Cindy Brogdon, UTK again placed third in 1979.

After the 1976 Olympics, Pat was elected to the council of the Amateur Basketball Association of the U.S.A. (ABAUSA), which began her tenure as an influential member within the political structure of international women's basketball. The ABAUSA coordinates and endeavors to improve women's and men's basketball in the United States. That year, Pat was one of two representative athletes on the 14-member council; 4 years later she was elected vice president for women, a post she still holds.

Pat's initial involvement with the ABAUSA offered her an opportunity to understand and participate in the powers that govern American international competition. No doubt this involvement was to a great extent responsible for her being selected in 1977 as head coach of the United States Junior National team.

Junior national teams are generally composed of players who are 19 years of age or younger. These high school seniors and college freshmen often form the nucleus for the Olympic team. Four of the players on Pat's 1977 junior team—Holly Warlick, Nancy Lieberman, Denise Curry, and Kris Kirchner—played together in various international tournaments during their undergraduate careers, then were selected for the 1980 Olympic team, but did not go because of the boycott.

Despite its young talent, that first junior national team was not expected to do well in its first international tournament, held in Squaw Valley, California. Yet they won the gold medal, compiling a 5-0 record. That accomplishment established Pat Summitt as a capable international coach.

Holly Warlick remembers one incident about the tournament that reflects a playful side of Pat Head Summitt. Warlick had developed a skin rash over her entire body, and Coach Summitt escorted her to the team physician. To determine the cause of the rash the doctor took a vial of blood from Warlick's arm.

Since Holly had never been ill, this was a new experience for the naive freshman from Tennessee. Pat told her that the blood test was necessary since several male hockey players, who were also competing at Squaw Valley, had tested positive for a venereal disease. The doctor, Pat said, wanted to make sure Holly had not been infected. Telling the story 10 years later, Warlick laughs. "Why, those hockey guys weren't even cute!"

After the Squaw Valley success, the same squad traveled in the early fall of 1977 to Mexico City for the Women's Pan American Confederation Tournament. Again to the surprise of the basketball world, the young Americans posted a 6-0 record for another gold medal.

After they won, the team members were grateful to their coach. But during pretournament conditioning, they were furious. To prepare for Mexico's high altitude, Summitt had the team run several miles twice a day for 3 weeks before the beginning of competition. Holly Warlick, a former track athlete and a Lady Vol, was used to Pat's demanding tactics, but she and the other players grumbled nevertheless. Only when they won did they reconsider that though Ms. Summitt might not be the nicest of coaches, she was one of the best.

International competition is always at its peak in the summer preceding an Olympic year. In the summer of 1979 the national women's basketball team played in three international competitions, and Pat coached them all.

For Summitt, the World Championship was the most memorable event of the summer of 1979. The games were played in a beautiful new 25,000-seat arena in Seoul, South Korea, and the facility was packed throughout the tournament. The American team lost their opening game but came back to win the gold medal by defeating Canada, 77-61.

The same United States team also participated in other tournaments that summer. Team members included Jill Rankin (UTK), Denise Curry (UCLA), Nancy Lieberman (ODU), Ann Meyers (UCLA), Carol Blazejowski (Montclair State), Holly Warlick (UTK), and Tara Heiss (Maryland).

Following the world championships, the American team traveled to Taipei where they competed in the Jones Cup tournament. There they were undefeated (6-0) and won another gold medal. But in their final tournament in 1979, the Pan Am Games in San Juan, they lost in the finals to Cuba and had to settle for a silver. Players and coaches were devastated. As Summitt said, "You don't win the World Championship and then lose in the Pan Ams."

In spite of the Pan American disappointment, Summitt's national team had accumulated an exceptional international record of 16 wins and 2 losses. Pat's coaching style had been effective regardless of her popular status with her players, and the ABAUSA, apparently equally pleased, named her assistant coach of the 1980 women's Olympic team.

Pat and head coach Sue Gunter had no idea that the United States would boycott the Moscow games. Neither coach dreamed that the Russian invasion of Afghanistan in December of 1979 would affect their Olympic aspirations. But in February of 1980, President Carter asked the International Olympic Committee either to move the games from the Russian capital or to postpone them until a later date. If the games were not moved or if the Soviets did not withdraw from Afghanistan, Carter warned, the United States would boycott the games.

Since neither of Carter's conditions was met, the United States Olympic Committee voted in April 1980 not to participate in the Moscow games. Japan, West Germany, Canada, and 62 other countries joined the Americans in support of the boycott. Great Britain sent a team in spite of the objections of their prime minister, Margaret Thatcher. When the British won the right to compete over government objections, American athletes hoped that they, too, might be able to participate. There were threats of court action, but in the end the Olympians supported President Carter.

Still, the American teams were permitted to participate in pre-Olympic qualifying tournaments. The tournament for women's basketball was held in Varna, Bulgaria, in May 1980. According to Olympic custom, the host country (in this instance, Russia) has an automatic invitation to the games and does not have to play in the qualifying round. So the Americans did not have an opportunity to compete against the powerful Russians, and won the qualifying tournament with a 5-1 record. Their only defeat was to Korea; the team had performed exceedingly well considering the circumstances. Coaches Gunter and Summitt had obviously done an outstanding job of motivating the team in spite of the overwhelming disappointment about not competing in Moscow.

Four members of that 1980 team—Denise Curry (UCLA), Anne Donovan (Old Dominion), Lynette Woodard (Kansas), and Cindy Noble (Tennessee)—later played on the 1984 Olympic team, realizing their Olympic dreams. For Holly Warlick and the other team members—Nancy Lieberman (Old Dominion), Jill Rankin (Tennessee), Carol Blazejowski (Montclair State), Kris Kirchner and Tara Heiss (Maryland), Rose Walker (Stephen F. Austin), Debra Miller (Boston University), and LaTaunya Pollard (Long Beach State)—amateur competition was over.

For Holly Warlick that end was particularly painful because it was also the end of a friendship. Warlick and Nancy Lieberman had played together for 4 years on international teams and had become close friends. After making the Olympic squad, Lieberman withdrew from the team and did not participate in the qualifying tournament in Bulgaria, telling the press that she had withdrawn to support President Carter. Warlick resented Lieberman's taking a spot on the team and then reneging on her obligation. Holly also questioned Nancy's motives. The Lady Vol athlete suspected that Lieberman, in addition to suffering a severe case of basketball burnout, was seeking publicity rather than following political convictions. Whatever the case, the friendship was another casualty of the 1980 Olympics.

To anyone familiar with international basketball, it came as no surprise that Pat Head Summitt was selected head coach of the 1984 Olympic squad. She had represented her country as an Olympic athlete, had coached successfully at all the important international competitions, and, finally, had been the assistant women's Olympic coach in 1980. Summitt was obviously well qualified for the job, as was her assistant, Kay Yow, North Carolina State's head coach. Nancy Darsch, Pat's longtime Tennessee assistant and now head coach at Ohio State, was chosen for the second assistant's position.

Selection of the 1984 Olympic team took 4 days. A total of 107 women took part in the tryouts, which were held at the Olympic training site in Colorado Springs, Colorado. Seventeen were chosen by the ABAUSA women's selection committee to form the nucleus of the Olympic squad; eventually only 12 would be included on the United States team. The remaining 5 would be named alternates, and would become Olympians only in the event the selected 12 would not be able to participate.

After the initial tryouts, the chosen 17 were sent home with instructions from Coach Summitt to maintain their conditioning; some were also told to lose weight. Upon their return to Colorado Springs 3 weeks later, the players had lost a total of 65 pounds.

Summitt's choice of the 17 was not without criticism. Tennessee fans in particular were upset that Mary Ostrowski, the Lady Vol all-American in 1981, '82, and '83, was cut. In March, preceding the April Olympic tryouts, Ostrowski had played brilliantly in the Final Four tournament, leading Tennessee to a second-place finish behind Southern Cal. Tennesseans found it difficult to understand how two other Lady Vols, Lea Henry and Cindy Noble, could have been selected over Mary O.

Summitt explained to the distressed fans that Ostrowski had been cut because her chronic foot and ankle problems might have prevented her from being effective in the fast-paced game of international basketball. According to Summitt, Ostrowski took the news well. Her parents, however, wrote Summitt an angry letter and called her to protest the decision.

Summitt says the decision to cut Mary unfortunately resulted in "a distance between us." Ostrowski graduated from UTK in 1985 and followed Nancy Darsch to Ohio State, where she has served since 1987 as an assistant coach to Darsch.

Upon their return to Colorado Springs, the 17 players practiced for 3 weeks before the 12-member Olympic squad was announced. Instead of informing players of their selection by posting jersey numbers (as had been the procedure for the 1976 and 1980 teams), Summitt called players individually into her office and gave them the good or bad news. The happy dozen included two Lady Vols—Cindy Noble ('77-'81) and Lea Henry ('79-'83)—as well as Teresa Edwards of Georgia; Anne Donovan (Old Dominion); Denise Curry (UCLA); Lynette Woodard (Kansas); Janice Laurence, the 1984 Wade Trophy winner from Louisiana Tech; Carol Menken-Schaudt (Oregon State); Cathy Boswell (Illinois State); Kim Mulkey, the 5-4 point guard also from Louisiana Tech; Pam McGee of

Southern California; and Southern California's Cheryl Miller, generally considered the best woman ever to play the game. Several of the women had spent a season or two playing in Europe or Japan, but because of a quirk in American eligibility rules, players such as Nancy Lieberman and Holly Warlick, who had played in the United States women's professional league, were ineligible for the Olympic participation.

Shortly after the selection of the Olympic squad, the team left for Taipei, Taiwan, where they easily won the Jones Cup. The most interesting occurrence at the Jones Cup was an incident involving Cheryl Miller. As soon as Miller's selection to the Olympic team was announced, there was speculation in the press concerning Summitt's ability to control the highly volatile USC superstar. When, early in the Taiwan competition, Miller objected to an official's call by slamming the basketball to the court, Summitt ended all speculation about the control of Ms. Miller. Cheryl was immediately removed from the game, and Summitt informed her that such behavior would not be tolerated. After that episode, there were no more problems with the star performer.

Nor were there problems with the rest of her star-studded team. Lynette Woodard, the Kansas all-American who established the NCAA women's scoring record and who later played for the Harlem Globetrotters, was quoted in the *Los Angeles Times* as saying, ''I've studied Pat and I know her mind. She works so hard and lives her values. I've tried to reflect that. She wants aggressive defense, no holding back. I don't fear her. I know the picture she wants to paint and I'm one of her tools. She can scream at me and I'll just listen to the message.'' The title of the article was ''A Despot Gone Soft.''

After returning from the Jones Cup, the Olympic team participated in a series of exhibition games against an all-star team composed of, among others, Nancy Lieberman, Carol Blazejowski, Nancy Dunkle, Heidi Wayment, and three former Tennessee athletes, Holly Warlick, Cindy Ely, and Debbie Groover. The culmination of the pre-Olympic competition was at the Hoosier Dome in Indianapolis where the women's team played the all-star team right before the men's Olympic team played a group of NBA all-stars. It was the first sellout for the new dome, and the 67,596 fans were not disappointed when both Olympic squads won.

From Indianapolis the team traveled to California to continue practicing for Olympic competition. There they scrimmaged against men's teams and suffered what was considered in some quarters a humiliating loss to a team composed of NBA rejects. Bobby Knight, the men's Olympic Coach, had advised Summitt against scheduling games against men's teams because

Knight felt losses to men's teams would be demoralizing to the women. Summitt, however, wanted to practice and play against tough opponents, and men's teams, by virtue of their size, strength, and quickness, provide the best competition for a female squad. So she ignored Knight's advice and scheduled scrimmages against men.

Perhaps those scrimmages contributed to their success. Also a contributing factor, says Pat, was their schedule. During 3 weeks of training in Long Beach, California, the team arose at 6:00 a.m., had breakfast at 6:15, and practiced at 9:00 a.m. The first Olympic game was scheduled at 9:00 in the morning against Yugoslavia, and Pat wanted the players to be ready. Pat had played in early morning games at the Montreal Olympics in 1976, and she thought the Amercians had not adjusted to playing at such an early hour.

Somehow, between good coaching, good players, and good preparation, everything worked. The Americans defeated Yugoslavia by 28 points (83-55), then went on to defeat China (91-55), Australia (81-47), South Korea (84-47), and Canada (92-61); and in the gold medal game, the Americans played South Korea for the second time and won by a score of 85-55. The silver medal went to South Korea with China winning the bronze.

Of course, this time the Soviets had boycotted. Still, a gold medal is a gold medal. The Americans were ecstatic, and soon the picture of the team carrying their head coach around the Los Angeles Forum was in newspapers around the world. Led by Lynette Woodard and Cheryl Miller, the United States team had been spectacular, and Coach Summitt had done a magnificent job of blending 12 outstanding individuals into a team of disciplined athletes.

Accolades to Summitt's coaching ability appeared in the national press and magazines, but her accomplishment was perhaps best expressed in an editorial in her hometown paper, the *Knoxville Journal*:

> The fact that she was the only woman among the head basketball coaches in the 1984 Olympics is probably significant to women and men alike—but not so widely understood is the fact that her skills and command of the sport would likely make her a title-contending coach in men's collegiate basketball, perhaps even in the professional game.
>
> Pat Summitt is, without qualification, one of those rare people to whom can be attached the proverbial description: "A winner in anybody's league."

CHAPTER NINE

Georgia on Their Minds

The Memphis State game is always more than a basketball contest. Although Memphis is approximately 400 miles from Knoxville, both cities are in Tennessee, and the universities are of almost equal size. When Tennessee travels to Memphis for any game there are always plenty of Big Orange alumni in the stands, and when Memphis State comes to Knoxville, Tiger fans follow in droves.

In fact, one of the reasons Tennessee enjoys playing in Memphis is that it gives west Tennessee alumni an opportunity to see the Vols in action, and provides a vehicle for members of the athletic department to maintain contact with the Big Orange Club of Memphis. When the Lady Vols came to town, for instance, the Big Orange Club held a pregame reception at a local racquet club, and Joan Cronan, women's athletic director, was invited to speak. Unfortunately, Joan missed her flight to Memphis, so Coach Summitt was asked to do the honors.

Summitt sent her team to the Memphis State Field House while she and assistant coaches DeMoss and Warlick and sports information director Debby Jennings hurried to the Big Orange Club reception. Pat thanked the alumni for their generosity and urged them to continue their support of their alma mater. She then mentioned that the few Tennessee fans who had been at the South Carolina game in Columbia had meant a lot to the Lady Vols. The way the head coach told the story, one would think those fans in Columbia won the game for Tennessee.

The point was not lost on Big Orange Club members. They scurried to the Memphis State Field House, arriving early so they could settle in directly behind the Tennessee bench. About one-fourth of the 2,800 fans were Lady Vol supporters. The Lady Tigers did not ordinarily fill the gymnasium, but for the Lady Vol game they staged their biggest promotion of the year: Everyone 18 and under who wore blue (one of the MSU school colors) was admitted free.

This particular Memphis State–Tennessee game was also special because the date, January 27, 1988, was junior guard Melissa McCray's 21st birthday. A popular team leader, McCray commanded respect from her teammates, perhaps following in the footsteps of her father, a minister. McCray wasn't afraid to criticize teammates whom she thought weren't working hard enough, and they in turn weren't afraid to mimic her effective but eccentric wind-mill style of defense. They nicknamed her "Emma" because they thought she acted like a mother, and Emma seemed to be a good name for an old lady. Though other team members had nicknames— "T" or "Ice" for Tonya, "Leggs" for injured player Carla McGhee, "Fat Dog" for Dawn Marsh—McCray was the one player who was consistently and affectionately called by her nickname. In honor of Emma's birthday, Coach Summitt allowed team members a small piece of cheesecake after their pregame meal, a departure from her usual no-desserts-before-games rule.

Like most of the Lady Vol opposition, Memphis State wanted to defeat the defending national champions more than they wanted to defeat any other team on their schedule. Trying to bring down the best is a powerful motivator, and this explains why many teams rise to the occasion. As the Memphis State coach Mary Lou Johns observed, "Many teams can play with Tennessee for 15 or 20 minutes, but after that their depth and talent become too much. They just wear teams down."

So it was on January 27. In the first half, the Memphis State players tenaciously denied Bridgette Gordon the ball, and trailed by only six points at halftime. Coach Summitt screamed at her team in the locker room, accusing them of not being aggressive enough. Early in the season, Pat pointed out, the Lady Vols had led the Southeastern Conference in number of steals, but in the last four games they had stolen the ball an average of five fewer times per game. Apparently, this bit of information was just what the Tennessee team needed to hear.

In the first 5 minutes of the second half, the Lady Vols intercepted passes and stole the ball from the startled Lady Tigers almost at will, raced down the court, and converted those steals into baskets. Before anyone knew what was happening, the score was 60-40, and by the end they dominated, 97-73.

Despite Memphis State's defensive efforts, Bridgette Gordon, who had been named Southeastern Conference Player of the Week for her performances against South Carolina and Alabama, again led the Lady Vols with 29 points. Dawn Marsh played her best game of the season with 11 points and 11 assists. Pearl Moore and Jennifer Tuggle contributed 12 and 9 points, respectively, and Kathy Spinks's excellent performance in 7 minutes of play indicated that she had fully recovered from her head injury. The birthday girl, Emma, also played well, scoring 8 points in 23 minutes.

To the chagrin of fans who were not able to attend in person, there was no radio coverage of the Lady Vol game because the UTK men's team was playing at the same time in Starkville, Mississippi, against Mississippi State. The Knoxville station that usually carries women's games, both home and away, was a part of the Vol radio network that gave priority to men's games. This was ironic since the Tennessee men's team was unranked, while the women were ranked fourth in the nation and were the defending national champions.

In spite of the lack of coverage, the Memphis State game was a fun trip. Three teammates who had played with Pat on the nearby UTM basketball team appeared at the game, and the stands were scattered with other friends and acquaintances. Mickie DeMoss, who had been an assistant under Mary Lou Johns at Memphis State, seemed to know everybody in the Field House. Pearl Moore also had friends and family in the crowd. Bridgette Gordon was particularly interested in the crowd because it included the parents of her boyfriend, Memphis native and Tennessee point guard Clarence Swearengen.

Three days later, the Lady Vols were back on the road, this time on their way to the University of Georgia. Again, it was old-home week for Coach Summitt, this time because her friend Jane Brown Clark was in Athens with her parents to cheer for the Lady Vols.

Jane has known Trish—as Pat Summitt is known to her family and childhood friends—since they played basketball together in seventh grade. "She is still my best friend," says Jane. "If I have something really bothering me, I want to share it with Trish."

Jane Clark lives in Clarksville, Tennessee, where she grew up and graduated from Austin Peay State University. Her background and lifestyle are typical of many American women. She married between her sophomore and junior years in college, completed her degree, had two children, and now teaches English in her hometown.

Trish has had a more atypical career, although remaining geographically close to her roots. The demands of her coaching responsibilities don't allow the Lady Vol mentor much time to spend in middle Tennessee with her own family or with Jane and other friends. But very different lifestyles have not diminished the Clark-Summitt friendship.

The two have always been different. Jane lived in town and Pat lived on a farm. Jane is an only child and, by her own admission, "spoiled rotten." Pat has three brothers and a sister and was anything but spoiled. According to Jane, "Trish accepted hard work. She milked, set tobacco, minded the store, baled hay, cooked, or did whatever needed to be done. She never had to be told. She just did it."

From Pat, Jane learned about responsibility and the value of hard work. Jane taught Pat grammar and how to dress. Jane maintains that without her, Pat would never be where she is today, especially in terms of public speaking. Jane remembers translating Shakespeare and writing English themes for Pat in both high school and college. "Isn't it ironic," she says now, "I taught Trish all she knows about English grammar; now she earns more speaking than I do teaching."

During their basketball playing days, Jane and Trish also had different roles. Girls' basketball in Tennessee was still a six-player game in Tennessee in the mid-sixties, and Jane played guard on one half of the court while Pat was the star forward on the other half. When Pat's family moved to nearby Cheatham County so she could continue her basketball career, Jane remained in town and went to the local public school. But Jane and Trish remained inseparable, and since they still did not live far apart, saw each other almost daily.

Pat was often left in charge of her parents' country store while Richard and Hazel attended to farm chores. Jane would visit, and when there were no customers, Pat and Jane would play card games such as "High Five." Trish wanted to be the best at everything, Jane remembers, and card-playing was no exception. She would never admit defeat, even at "High Five."

The Head country store carried a variety of merchandise in addition to groceries, including hardware supplies and a line of clothes for men, women, and children. Jane and Pat made numerous clothes-buying excursions to Nashville to supply the store; this afforded Jane an opportunity to teach Pat about style.

The girls tried smoking cigarettes, but as they were good Methodists, drugs and alcohol were out of the question. Their most mischievous deed was painting the city water tower. They didn't even do it themselves—they just aided and abetted—but the risk was great because Richard Head was the county water commissioner. That night they slept at Pat's house.

The next morning at breakfast, Mr. Head, obviously agitated, told the girls about the desecration of the water tower, and said to the two teenagers, "I know you all know everything that goes on around here. Find out who did this dirty trick and let me know. They must be punished." Neither Trish nor Jane said a word, but Jane still remembers the bruise she received from Pat's strong kicks under the table. According to Jane, "Richard Head does not know, to this day, who the culprits were."

Jane believes that Richard Head was the most influential person in Pat's life. "Trish always wanted his approval, and even today when she calls me after a game, she never fails to ask, 'What did Daddy think?' "

Jane's wedding was another occasion for mischief. Pat was Jane's maid of honor and as such was there to help her childhood buddy through all the fun and frustrations of getting married. Not surprisingly, Pat added to the frustration by finding the key to Jane's going-away luggage, filling the suitcase with rice, stealing all her underwear, and tying her first-night negligee into a thousand knots. Jane was near tears when she discovered this upon arrival at the honeymoon motel. Now, 15 years later, she can laugh about it, and admits one of the bridesmaids foiled one of Pat's tricks by handing Jane a paper sack with her underwear in it as she and her new husband drove away from the reception.

Jane was an attendant in Pat's wedding several years later, but Pat's husband, R.B., ever suspicious, hid their luggage and prevented Jane from reciprocating.

The two couples have remained close over the years. This past summer 12-year-old Chris Clark, Jane's oldest son, worked at the Pat Head Summitt Basketball Camp on the UTK campus. Jane had some misgivings about Chris's working at the camp, fearing he would be homesick, or worse yet, lazy. Pat assured Jane that her son was a wonderful worker. Said Pat, "You know I was harder on him because he belongs to you, Jane, but he responded beautifully."

Together in Athens, Georgia, before the Georgia-Tennessee game, Jane and Pat's closeness was immediately apparent. As they sat around a table with other Lady Vol staff members and supporters, they laughed and talked with each other about all kinds of things besides basketball. This didn't last long, however. Shortly someone interrupted the conversation: "Pat, you're wanted on the telephone. It's the press."

When Tennessee plays Georgia, Coach Summitt and Coach Andy Landers match wits and strategies in such fierce competition that the struggle between the two head coaches can be more fascinating to watch than the actual game. The media, of course, feeds such rivalries. The Athens newspaper, for example, quoted Andy as saying that Tennessee was Georgia's biggest game, whereas Pat was quoted in the same article as saying that the Lady Vol's biggest game was against whoever was Number 1. At the time, Georgia was ranked 13. Pat's insistence that the Bulldog contest was just another game had angered Andy, according to the press, and this most recent conflict fueled the fire.

The rivalry between the coaches is natural since both are Tennesseans, both coach at Southeastern Conference schools, both recruit the same players, and both have beaten each other at crucial times in the Mideast regional tournament. Plus, both coaches are intense competitors. Evidence of Landers's intensity is the lack of red paint in front of the Lady Bulldog bench. His incessant pacing during games has worn the finish completely off the floor.

Tennessee arrived in Athens on Saturday, just in time for their 5:30 p.m. practice. The session lasted about an hour, and then the team retired to the Holiday Inn. After considering the options of eating at a local restaurant or having pizzas sent to their rooms, the players voted for the pizza. Eating in their rooms would allow more time for relaxation and studying. A 2-hour study hall was mandated, but most of the women did not need the mandate. They were eager to hit the books since they were in the midst of a five-game road series, and midterm exams were coming up in 2 weeks. No one had missed classes for the Sunday afternoon Georgia game, but next week they would not be in class on Wednesday and Thursday because of the Notre Dame trip, and the following week they would be absent from Monday and Tuesday classes for games against Ole Miss and Mississippi State.

The Tennessee-Georgia game day—Sunday, January 31, 1988—also happened to be Super Bowl Sunday. One year, when Tennessee had scheduled a home Lady Vol game in conflict with Super Bowl Sunday, the game was rescheduled (the Lady Vol game, not the Super Bowl!). This year, since the basketball game was scheduled for 2:30 p.m. and the Super Bowl for 6:15 p.m., Georgia fans would not have to make a choice, but a busload of Tennessee supporters and the Lady Vol official party would miss the Super Bowl. Since the Denver Broncos–Washington Redskins game ended in a 42-10 rout by Washington, sport fans would have been treated to a much better game between the women's basketball teams of Georgia and Tennessee.

Before the game, Pat huddled with her coaches to give them their assignments. Holly was instructed to concentrate on the Tennessee defense, Mickie on the Tennessee offense, and graduate assistant, Heidi Van Derveer, on the Georgia offense. Then Pat said, "I hear Andy's going to start five freshmen. Can you believe that?" Summitt continued, "If he starts five freshmen they'll be intimidated." The other coaches laughed when their boss said, "Can't you hear those Georgia rookies asking, 'Guard Bridgette who?' "

In the locker room, Pat instructed her team, "Let's have 30 seconds of mental practice. Everybody close your eyes and concentrate on ways you can help win this game." At the end of the imagery session, Pat said simply, "We're better than Georgia. Don't worry about them. Do your best and we'll win."

The game had an added dimension since it was being televised in Knoxville and student assistant, Shelley Sexton, was the color analyst along with commentator Bob Kesling. This was Sexton's first TV experience in such a role.

But Shelley knew basketball, and she knew these teams. She had been captain of the previous year's team, and was now serving as an assistant coach while completing her requirements for a bachelor's degree in physical education. Like all Lady Vols who are unable to graduate in 4 years, Shelley was being given an athletic scholarship for an additional year.

Her responsibilities included monitoring study hall, assisting with scouting reports, and taking care of whatever organizational details might be necessary. But because the squad was small and occasionally plagued by injuries, Shelley often scrimmaged with the players during practice. Like Shelia Collin's postcard, Shelley Sexton's presence served as a reminder of the glory of the past and motivated the current players to again claim the national championship. Her invitation to act as color commentator further inspired them, proving that opportunities would await them after they left the team.

To the surprise of the Lady Vol coaching staff, Landers did indeed start five freshmen. His strategy seemed to pay off: They were highly motivated, had few turnovers, and played together as though they had been teammates for years. Coach Summitt had been wrong about intimidation. The frosh Lady Bulldogs showed no signs of backing off from the national champions.

The Lady Vol team, on the other hand, seemed disconcerted by Coach Landers as he marched up and down the sidelines, shouting to his team using Tennessee terms such as "Big Orange" and "Tennessee Four" for Georgia's offensive and defensive sets. Nevertheless, Tennessee led at halftime by a score of 43-39.

At intermission, Pat's emphasis was on rebounding. "Anybody backs off on the boards, you can sit!" she warned. "Good job handling the full-court pressure," she added, and to Sheila, who had hit nine for nine from the field and three for three from the free throw line, simply, "Good job, Sheila." As the team left the dressing room the head coach reminded them, "The first 3 minutes of the second half are the most important; that tells who wants the ball game."

They all yelled, "Let's go."

The Lady Vols came storming out after the half, but could build the lead to no more than five points. With about 6 minutes remaining, Georgia went ahead by three. The 2,000 fans, most of whom were Bulldogs, went wild. Coach Summitt called time. The Lady Vols regrouped, and, not to be outdone by the Georgia freshmen, the Lady Vol rookies helped their team surge ahead. Pearl got an offensive rebound and went back up for two points at a crucial time, and Kris scored two buckets from long range to keep the Lady Vols in the game. One of the prettiest plays in the game was when Pearl executed a screen-and-roll to the basket and Kris fed her a perfect pass. Unfortunately, Moore missed the easy lay-up.

Coach Landers may also inadvertently have scored one point for Tennessee. In his usual pose of both arms extended high overhead, he was signaling for the Georgia fans to cheer louder. But both arms extended high overhead is also the signal for a three-point goal. When Bridgette Gordon hit a long jumper, the officials, confused by the noisy crowd, seemed unsure as to whether it was a three-pointer. It wasn't. But when they saw Lander's signal, they raised their hands and awarded the Lady Vols three points. Nobody from Georgia (or from Tennessee) objected. That put Tennessee ahead by five points and was a turning point in the game. With a few seconds remaining, Tonya Edwards was fouled while attempting a shot and made both free throws, sealing the Tennessee victory, 82-79.

When the two coaches met in the center of the court for the hand-shaking ritual, the contrast was striking. Landers was totally disheveled.

His coat had been removed and his tie was askance, his sleeves shoved carelessly above his elbows. Summitt, in a trim tan suit, was the picture of composure. She might have been on her way to a garden party.

To celebrate the win, the cheerleaders, who had traveled to Georgia with the team, gave a special cheer when the team got on the bus. The Lady Vols reciprocated with a "hip, hip, hooray" for the women and men who cheer them on. It was a bus full of happy campers.

The 5-hour return to Knoxville was pleasant not only because Tennessee won, but because Holly Warlick brought a small portable TV set; the avid football fans crowded around Holly for peeks at the Super Bowl. Most of the interested onlookers were cheering for Washington and the first black Super Bowl quarterback, Doug Williams, so the Redskin victory made it a double sweep and an especially happy sports day for the Lady Vols.

The team arrived back at Stokely around 10:30 p.m. The Super Bowl had lasted almost the entire trip so the team was still celebrating that victory as they left the bus. Before the team departed, Mickie DeMoss gave instructions for the following week: No Monday practice, but all Lady Vols were scheduled for weight lifting and for a film session of the Georgia game; practice would resume at the usual time on Tuesday, with departure for the airport and the flight to Notre Dame immediately after the workout. No rest for the weary.

CHAPTER TEN

A Tennessee Tradition

The month of February 1988 began, as it usually does, with a debate over whether the groundhog in Punxsutawney, Pennsylvania, had seen its shadow. Weather reporter Willard Scott said the sun did not shine anywhere in the United States on February 2, making shadows impossible, but newspaper accounts indicated just the opposite: lots of sunshine. And the best source, the groundhog itself, was not telling.

For the Lady Vols, weather reports were important because of their upcoming trips to South Bend, Indiana, and then Mississippi for three road games. Bad weather can mean flight delays or cancelations, and can affect the number of fans who attend games. As it turned out, a light snow slowed them down, but, after the game, provided an opportunity for fun.

Most of the team flew from Knoxville to Chicago on the Tuesday before the Wednesday game with Notre Dame. Due to flight delays and a rental car mix-up, they did not arrive in South Bend, Indiana, until 2:00 in the morning on Wednesday. Sheila, Tonya, Bridgette, and graduate assistant Heidi Van Derveer left Knoxville at 8:20 Wednesday morning and joined the team just in time for the pregame meal.

For once, the team was introduced as the Tennessee Volunteers, instead of the Lady Vols, and Notre Dame called themselves simply the Fighting Irish, instead of using any feminization of that name. The players also noticed something else unusual: All of the the Notre Dame players were white.

Notre Dame had been undefeated at home that season, and in the first half, they looked like they might keep that record. Their two post players were particularly effective inside, and held Sheila Frost to only two baskets in four attempts. Needless to say, Summitt had some words with Frost at halftime. She also gave the entire team, as they say in the South, "what for."

Though Tennessee led 45-37, Summitt gave not a single word of praise. "You all, we're giving up too many points," she said. "Last year in the national championship game, Louisiana Tech scored only 44 in the whole game. Come on, get with it!" Then she appealed to their Tennessee pride. "Don't you know what it means to wear the orange? Some of you don't play like it. Quit being concerned with your own game and be concerned for Tennessee!"

Again, her pep talk seemed to work wonders. They shot an amazing 66 percent from the field, with Bridgette hitting 13 of 15 shots and Jennifer scoring 6 buckets for a final score of 91-71.

Coach Summitt praised her team afterward, and appeared to be in a great mood, even relatively relaxed. That was not the impression, however, that she gave the Irish fans.

Concerned that the team was losing its conditioning, which often happens midseason since road trips and games interfere with practice time, Pat gave the players the choice of running wind sprints immediately after the game or having a regular practice the next day. They chose the wind sprints, and Pat received permission from Notre Dame officials to use the gym for 30 minutes of postgame running.

As they slowly filed out of the gymnasium, Notre Dame fans were appalled to see the Lady Vols engaged in strenuous wind sprints. They couldn't comprehend why a team that had just won by 20 points would be punished like this. During a brief break, one of them whispered to Jennifer, "Is your coach mad?" Tuggle, who later told the story to Pat, responded, "No, she's in a good mood. You should see her mad!"

But the running looked fun or perhaps challenging to six male Notre Dame cheerleaders, who asked Pat if they could run with her squad. The men ran strongly in the beginning, but one by one they dropped out. At the end of 30 minutes, only one remained. Kathy Spinks observed to no one in particular, "At last, one real man. And he's cute!"

As planned, the Lady Vols left immediately after practice for the 2-1/2-hour drive back to Chicago. Snow had continued to fall all afternoon, and conditions might be worse by morning.

With Holly driving one rental van, Mickie another, and Pat a rental car, the 16-member Lady Vol party began the slow caravan journey over the snow-covered interstate to the windy city. On the outskirts of South Bend, they stopped at Arby's for sandwiches. It was then that Pat noticed Sheila's beach attire: sandals and no coat! "But Pat!" Sheila defended herself. "It was 70 degrees in Knoxville when I left this morning." Then, exaggerating her southern accent, she added, "We just don't have this kind of weather in Pulaski, Tennessee."

After the Arby's snack, the players riding with Pat were treated to a doughnut—not the junk food kind, but the parking lot kind. "Want to see a doughnut?" Pat said to Bridgette, who was sitting in the front seat with her. The Floridian didn't know what Pat was talking about, but that didn't matter to Pat. She stepped on the accelerator, turned the wheel sharply, and skidded in a perfect circle on the snow and ice. Pat loved it. Even head coaches can't resist being kids when it comes to snow.

On the drive to Chicago, the players in Pat's car talked mostly about dating. They also asked Pat about her many trips abroad. Pat said Budapest had been her favorite city, and that she was eager to return to New Zealand. Basketball talk was at a minimum, but someone mentioned that it had been strange to play against the all-white Notre Dame team. Pat responded, "There is a difference in coaching black and white kids. Black kids are so much less inhibited. They are so honest." Then she added, "But both black and white basketball players are temperamental and hard to coach." When the car was silent, she turned to Bridgette and said, "Right, Bridgette?" Everyone laughed.

Because of the snow, the caravan did not reach the motel, 8 miles from O'Hare Airport, until 3:00 in the morning. Arriving anywhere at that hour is stressful, but entering a freezing hotel room can be particularly depressing. Pat hurriedly assigned the players two to a room and everyone went quickly to bed. Wake-up would be at 8:30 in the morning.

The short night over, the assembled team drove to the airport. There had been no time for breakfast, but a snack on the plane was promised. Snack it was: one small bagel and three miniature slices of melon. The players grumbled and scarfed down the food. Pat promised them food in Atlanta, but this was impossible; there was only an 18-minute layover between flights, and they had to sprint through the airport to make the connection. Someone said, "Pat should have counted this as conditioning instead of making us run last night."

Starved, the Lady Vols arrived in Knoxville at 2:10 p.m., but still they could not eat until they got back to campus. After eating, most would rush to appointments with faculty advisors since spring registration would end tomorrow, and after tomorrow's classes they would be on the road again for games against Ole Miss and Mississippi State.

Since flying to Oxford, Mississippi, is virtually impossible, the bone-weary Lady Vols flew instead to Memphis, where they were met by a chartered bus that drove them the final 70 minutes to their destination. In the opening 10 minutes of the game at the University of Mississippi, Ole Miss raced to a 24-10 lead. But the Lady Vols woke up eventually to claim a 78-67 victory.

For most, this was just another game in what had become a long series of games. But for Dawn Marsh, the game marked a milestone: She broke the Lady Vol career assist record previously held by Holly Warlick. By making six passes to teammates who scored as a result of those passes, Marsh finished the game with 674 career assists, one more than the Tennessee coach. Holly congratulated her afterward, teasing, "Dawn learned everything from me."

After the Ole Miss victory, the Lady Vols returned to their motel rooms and collapsed. After four successful road games, they were exhausted. Because of their obvious fatigue, the coaches decided to keep the team in Oxford on Friday and Saturday night, then leave for Starkville on Sunday for the Monday night contest against Mississippi State. But there would be no time for excursions to the countryside William Faulkner made famous in his stories about fictitious Yoknapatawhpa County. The Lady Vols needed to study, and, primarily, to rest.

Included in the entourage that was making its way from hotel to hotel, game to game, was an unsung hero named Laura Craig. As the head manager for the Lady Vols, Laura Craig could not rest or study when the team had time off. Uniforms and towels needed to be washed, water bottles needed to be filled, everything needed to be packed and ready for the game. Then it had to be lifted and carried. "The Number 1 requirement for this job should be strength," says Laura. "It takes a Samson to carry those heavy duffel bags long distances."

Laura, a high school basketball player in Stewart County, Tennessee, took on the role of assistant manager in her freshman year of 1986, but this year, when the head manager was relieved of her duties early in the season, Laura received a "battlefield" promotion, so to speak. Karen Durham, sister of freshman point guard, Kris Durham, was appointed Laura's assistant.

Laura does not have a written job description, but her responsibilities include helping Holly Warlick plan the itinerary and making room assignments for away games. The managers' primary responsibilities, though, are providing assistance at practices and games.

During practice, the managers record shooting percentages, keep the game clock for scrimmages and drills, and are available for any emergency that may arise. As Laura explains, "We have to be ready with whatever the coaches and players need, and it really helps if we can anticipate those needs."

Well before the athletes arrive, Laura and Karen have the practice uniforms ready. In addition, towels and water bottles are available for each player, and equipment such as balls and pinnies are in the gymnasium by the time the coaches and players appear.

Games provide other challenges. Laura prefers home games because she doesn't have to miss classes, but they can be time-consuming since either she or Karen must attend the opponent's practice the night before the contest to provide any needed help. On game day both managers arrive 2 hours early to take care of the necessary details. This includes providing towels and other amenities for the opponent's and officials' dressing rooms.

Packing for an away game—or rather the lack of packing—has been one of Laura's most memorable experiences as a manager. Careful though they were, the managers neglected to pack Bridgette Gordon's uniform on a trip in 1987 to Alabama, where the women were playing a preliminary game to the Crimson Tide versus Tennessee men's game. Bridgette borrowed a uniform from the Tennessee men's team, but the head manager was responsible for mistakes of this sort, so Laura's predecessor was subsequently replaced.

A more recent incident had a happier ending. Due to a scheduling problem, the Lady Vols were practicing in the physical education building rather than in the arena. When this occurred, the basketballs had to be transported from one building to the other. The two managers had gotten the balls to the PE gym without difficulty, but returning them to the equipment room in Stokely was another matter. They decided to put the balls, along with the ball rack, in the trunk of Karen's car, and since it was only a couple of blocks to Stokely, to leave the trunk up. That was a mistake. No sooner had they pulled away from the curb than basket-balls, rack and all, were pouring onto the street.

Laura and Karen were frantic. They jumped from the car and gathered the elusive balls as quickly as possible. They then began to laugh. This slowed down the retrieval process considerably, especially when they reached for the cart and discovered it had lost one of its wheels. Hilarious!

Still weak from laughter, they managed to scoop up the remaining balls and the damaged cart and return everything to Stokely Athletics Center. Just another day's work, according to Laura.

Laura said one of the greatest rewards of being a team manager was getting to know the players and coaches. One player she knew well was Sheila Frost, her roommate. When asked whether Sheila ever got depressed by Coach Summitt's continued badgering of the 6-4 center, Laura replied, "No, she really doesn't. Sheila knows she's sometimes lazy and needs to be yelled at."

Laura Craig didn't need to be yelled at. "I genuinely enjoy doing this," she said. "It's certainly not for the money." Nobody could argue with that, since the salary was not enough to cover the cost of tuition.

In regard to Laura's relationship with the head coach, the manager said, "Like everybody else, I really respect Pat, and consider it a privilege to work for her. I get to see a different side of her than the players do. More relaxed. More fun."

The UTK women and all their equipment arrived in Starkville, Mississippi, on Sunday afternoon, and since game time was not until Monday night, they had lots of time to kill. The waiting was beginning to be a nightmare for players, coaches, and managers alike. Everybody was bored, and bore-dom combined with tiredness can lead to petty bickering. Thank heavens, thought Coach Summitt, for VCRs. The coaching staff rented several videos, and all were invited to the coaches' suite to watch the films on the VCR.

Once on the court, the Lady Vols escaped with another victory, 81-74. In Mississippi's 10,000-seat Humphreys Coliseum, the official attendance was recorded as 179. Summitt, maintaining that the figure was inflated, was quoted in the newspaper: "They must have counted everyone there, including the teams. . . . You'd think they would come out to see the defending national champions, but they wouldn't necessarily have been entertained by our performance tonight." The article went on to explain that Mississippi State does not usually play on Monday nights, and that

"Alf," a favorite television show, was apparently too much competition for women's basketball.

But the players were jubilant. They had not played particularly well, but they had survived another road game, and had increased their road record to 12-0. Also, they were on their way back to the new arena, where they were averaging 7,668 fans per game.

Five days later, the Louisiana State game pitted Sue Gunter, in her 6th season as head coach at LSU, against Summitt, in her 14th season at UTK. The two friends had enjoyed a long association, first when Gunter coached Middle Tennessee State University and Summitt was a player at UTM; then when Sue helped coach the 1976 Olympic team that Pat co-captained; then again in 1980, when Gunter was head coach of the Olympic team and Pat, by then an established coach herself, was Sue's assistant.

Sue's friendship extended to Pat's parents as well, and when she entered the Thompson-Boling Arena she immediately spied Hazel and Richard Head in the front row and walked over to them to offer hugs and handshakes. Sue's next stop was the Tennessee bench, where she and Pat slapped hands. "Good luck," they said simultaneously.

Tennessee defeated Louisiana State, but only by a score of 89-82. Summitt praised Spinks, Tuggle, McCray, Durham, and Edwards, but expressed dismay with the overall Tennessee defense. "LSU scored 82 points on us," she reminded the players. " I can't believe it. If we don't play better against La Tech, we're going to get our behinds beat." After a pause, she continued, "Are we getting complacent? Do we need to get beat? Sometimes teams do, you know." She dismissed her charges with "12:30 curfew. Practice tomorrow [Sunday] from 2:00 to 4:00. Get some rest." On her way out the door, Holly Warlick added, "If you don't get out of this complacency, you're going to get blown away."

But in the game against "La Tech," as the Louisiana school is known in the south, Tennessee didn't get blown away. Ben Byrd, sports editor of the *Knoxville Journal*, described it this way:

It was a storybook game with a storybook ending. The best basket-ball contest played in Thompson-Boling Arena in the first season of its existence.

It had all the ingredients that it takes to make a game a classic. The winner and the runner-up for last year's national championship. A great crowd. Hard-nosed play, with an occasional scuffle here and there. A long, uphill climb by the home team. And, to cap it off, the winning shot at the buzzer.

It also had sacrifice. In the practice before the game, Pearl Moore had wrenched her knee, and she sat through the game with two crutches by her side.

And revenge: Sheila Frost was paired against their 6-4 star center, Venus Lacy, who had been her rival in high school. Lacy, from Chattanooga, had been recruited by the Lady Vols. But she chose Old Dominion over Tennessee, and went there her freshman year. Unhappy at ODU, Lacy contacted Pat about the possibility of transferring to UTK, but by then Pat wasn't interested, so Lacy transferred to Louisiana Tech.

At the beginning of the game, Lacy and her teammate, 6-3 Erica Westbrooks, scored almost at will, hitting short jumpers from inside the paint while all-American Teresa Weatherspoon directed an almost flawless Tech offense. Frost, in a desperate effort to comply with Summitt's directive to "be tough," got into a shoving match with Lacy that had to be broken up by the referee. Frost and Lacy tapped hands to indicate no real animosity, and the game continued without further incident.

Frost finally got her chance for stardom at the end: With 3:28 remaining, Bridgette intercepted a pass, dribbled the length of the court, and made the lay-up, giving Tennesee their first lead, 68-67. This one-point difference seesawed back and forth, and with 7 seconds left, the score was tied at 74. Tech was forced to shoot as time ran out on their 30-second shot clock, and Gordon was fouled as she grabbed the rebound.

Before the one-and-one free throw, Coach Summitt asked the Lady Vol if she would like a time-out for a moment's rest. Gordon declined and stepped to the free throw line. After taking a deep breath, which everyone in the arena could hear, Bridgette released the ball. It arched high but dropped just short of the hole, bouncing off the front rim, off the fingers of Melissa McCray, and into the hands of a startled Dawn Marsh. Marsh dribbled twice, looked at the bucket, then spotted Sheila Frost. She bounced the ball to Frost, who caught it, turned, and banked the 2-foot shot. The buzzer sounded, the scoreboard flashed 76-74, and Lady Vols started leaping around the court. The 7,000 fans went wild.

Pat's husband, R.B., was one of the first on the floor to share the moment with his wife. After giving her a kiss, he hugged all the members of the team. Pat, too, was ecstatic. She had hugs for all the Lady Vols, and a special pat on the head for Sheila.

The Lady Vol locker room was absolute bedlam. As Pat entered the noisy sanctuary, she looked at one of the guest coaches, winked, and said, "Can you believe that finish?" Everyone cheered. Besides a heartfelt congratulations, Pat had no other comments. There was so much joy, excitement, and relief that words had become superfluous. Pat mingled with well-wishers, then left to make comments on the postgame radio show. "Enjoy your victory," she said to her team. There was no mention of a curfew.

The next day, Pat met with her team on Tom Black Track. Instead of regular practice, the Lady Vols had a workout under the watchful eye of conditioning coach Whitey Hitchcock. After the mile run, the head coach called the team over to the bleachers and asked Whitey, "How was it?" "They gave a good effort," said Whitey.

"I'm proud of how you respond to the conditioning aspects of the program," Summitt told her players. "I think it helped us win last night. La Tech was definitely tired in the last 5 minutes. We weren't."

Summitt then became somber as she told the Lady Vols about Pearl Moore's knee. They had all seen Pearl's crutches at the game, but she hadn't told them the extent of the injury. "Pearl's going to have surgery next Tuesday," Pat said. "She has a torn ACL [anterior cruciate ligament]." The head coach then added quietly, "She's going to need your help now more than ever. I know you'll give it to her."

The injury could have been predicted—and was, to some extent. Since maintaining leg strength is extremely important for preventing knee injuries, basketball players are tested on the Cybex machine at least three times: preseason, midseason, and postseason. Jenny Moshak, the trainer, monitored the Cybex procedure carefully and prescribed exercises and weight-lifting programs for athletes whose legs were weak. Moshak had been concerned about Pearl Moore's lack of leg strength. So she was disappointed, but not surprised, to hear of the season-ending injury.

Reviewing the Louisiana Tech game, Pat praised the great effort by Jennifer Tuggle. Her teammates clapped in agreement. Summitt also had high praise for Kris Durham for an outstanding performance and said Durham and Tuggle were responsible for the great depth of the Tennessee team; they came off the bench and made contributions not only against the Techsters, but throughout the season.

Several team members had spent their free time escorting high school students around campus lately, and Pat thanked them for helping her with recruiting efforts. "I didn't know you had it in you, Kris, great job. If Karemma Williams doesn't come to Tennessee, it's not your fault. It's the staff's fault." Williams, from Michigan, was one of the Lady Vols' most sought-after recruits. Another one of those recruits, 6-1 Debbie Hawhee, from Greenville, Tennessee, had verbally committed to UTK at the game last night, Pat told her team.

Vicki Hall, the choice recruit from Indianapolis, had turned Pat down, choosing instead to sign with the University of Texas. Unless asked, this was not the sort of thing Pat announced at team meetings; better to stick to good news. But privately, Mickie DeMoss had related to Pat a humorous yet poignant story. Hall had made her decision in November, shortly after her visits to Tennessee, Iowa, and Texas. In January, Vicki's mother had called DeMoss, asking, "Why don't you phone anymore?" Mickie explained to the neglected mother that since Vicki had decided on Texas, the Tennessee contacts were over. Mrs. Hall expressed great regret and told DeMoss, "I feel as though I have lost a good friend."

After the discussion about recruits, Kerry Howland gave the players an academic pep talk. "We've got to work on those grades," she said. "Just as you didn't fold last night, you can't fold now with those grades." Howland was concerned because winter quarter grades would be given before some of the postseason tournaments, and several Lady Vols would be academically ineligible if their grades did not improve.

Pat singled out Dawn. "Dawn Marsh, if you're the first Lady Vol not to graduate, you will embarrass me, the program, your family, and most of all, yourself," she said sternly.

Then Pat gave them the schedule for the next few days, and warned them that their next opponent, the University of Kentucky, would love to win. "You know beating Tennessee would make Kentucky's season, and we're not making anybody's season," she said.

The team responded in unison, "You got that right!"

Usually Summitt preferred not to have her team travel on game days, but her players had missed more than the usual number of classes this season, and the head coach was concerned that this might be causing the grade problems. So she made plans to travel to and from Kentucky on the same day. The Lady Vols left for Lexington at noon on February 18, after morning classes, and arrived at 3:00. They then rested in a suite at the Marriott Hotel, ate the usual pregame pizza, and left at 6:15 for the 7:30 tip-off.

The Kentucky women were particularly eager to defeat Tennessee since both their coaches knew Pat well. Head coach Sharon Fanning had been Summitt's assistant in 1976 while completing her master's degree in physical education at UTK. Cindy Noble Hauserman, Fanning's assistant, had been one of Pat's stars during her undergraduate career (1978-81), and had later played on several of Pat's international teams, including the 1984 Olympic team. They wanted nothing more than to show their former mentor just how much they had learned.

As was becoming their pattern, Tennessee dragged in the first half, leading by only one point, 35-34. Kentucky's junior guard, Jodie Whitaker, played brilliantly, driving through the lane, sinking short jumpers, and handing off the ball to teammates who were in a position to score.

"Can anyone guard Jodie Whitaker?" Summitt pleaded at halftime. When no one answered, she challenged Melissa McCray, "How about you, Melissa?"

In a quiet voice, McCray said, "Okay."

Summitt also accused Dawn Marsh of laziness. "Are you tired? Is your season over?"

"No!" said Dawn loudly.

"You're not playing with your usual intensity," said Summitt.

After halftime, Dawn played with more than her usual intensity, scoring 9 of her 11 points and adding seven assists. It was one of her best 20-minute segments as a Lady Vol.

Lisa Webb, who had been replaced in the starting lineup by Jennifer Tuggle, also had a fine game, scoring 14 points and snagging nine rebounds. Tuggle, in her first start of the season, also satisfied the coach, and Tennessee won easily, 99-75. But in her postgame remarks, Summitt said, "Again you played well for 20 minutes. That was good enough to win tonight, but it won't be enough in postseason games."

On the return trip to Knoxville, Summitt announced the schedule for the rest of the week: no practice tomorrow (Friday), but there would be a weight-lifting session at noon. Saturday practice would be at 10:00 a.m. The team preferred an earlier practice time, but Summitt said she couldn't be there before 10:00. She was flying to Nashville after Friday's practice to accept the Amateur Athlete of the Year Award on behalf of the Lady Vols. The award was being given by the Tennessee Sports Hall of Fame, which was also honoring Summitt. They named her Tennessean of the Year.

The team stopped briefly at Wendy's, and then headed south, arriving back at Stokely at 1:30 a.m. For Pat, sports information director Debby Jennings, and Bridgette Gordon, the trip had been especially tiring. Because they had made an appearance at the Women's Basketball Media Day in

Number 34 Lisa Webb vs. Florida

New York the previous day, they had gotten up at 5:30 a.m. to catch a flight from New York to Lexington. The exhausting schedule did not hurt Bridgette's performance, however. She had scored a game-high 21 points and had eight rebounds in just 25 minutes of play.

Of all the promotional gimmicks, the favorite among Lady Vol fans is called "Drive Away a Giveaway." In this contest, auto dealers donate used cars and as the fans enter the arena, they register to win these preowned beauties. During time-outs throughout the game, Smokey, the Tennessee mascot, draws names, and Bobby Denton, well known by UTK fans as the public address announcer at football games, announces the winners.

In 1988, the "Drive Away a Giveaway" promotion fell on the Lady Vols' game with the University of Florida on February 21. Eight cars and one truck were raffled. Before reading the name of the winner, Denton would describe the car: "Here we have a 1977 Granada, yellow in color, four-door (two of which open), with 141,460 wonderful miles driven by a little old lady to Lady Vol games." He added with a chuckle, "To Lady Vol games everywhere." As the "lucky" winner was announced, Denton shouted into the microphone, "Wrecker service is available."

The game itself was a rout. Bridgette Gordon came down with the flu the night before and did not play, but Tennessee still managed to demolish Florida, 108-53. Of the eight Lady Vols who were able to play, seven scored in double figures, and Kris Durham scored nine. Leading Tennessee was Lisa Webb, with 21 points and 14 rebounds. For the second game in a row, Tuggle had started instead of Webb, but Lisa was spectacular coming off the bench.

Tonya Edwards, who started for Gordon, also had a great game, with 20 points, 12 rebounds, and eight steals. Coach Summitt was thrilled. "It was a fun game. I loved it!" she said afterward.

For Florida, there was one big moment. That came early in the evening, during introductions, when the announcer said, "Let's welcome former Olympian and all-time great Lady Vol, Lea Henry." The crowd responded with a thunderous ovation. Henry, who played at UTK during 1979-83, is now an assistant coach at Florida.

The last away game, against the University of North Carolina, also featured a former Lady Vol. Trish Roberts, now an assistant coach at UNC, had played for Pat at UTK from 1977 to 1981, and with Pat on the 1976 Olympic team. North Carolina's head coach, Sylvia Rhyne Hatchell, was also an old friend, having coached Summitt's junior varsity team at Tennessee in 1974, Pat's first year at the Lady Vol helm.

In preparation for the game and also for postconference play, Summitt spent considerable practice time working on a 1-2-2 zone defense. "Our opponents will not be expecting us to play a zone," she explained, "but we'll need it to prevent inside passes to those big post players. Auburn, Texas, La Tech, and Georgia killed us on that." She went on to tell the team that she and her assistants had discussed the zone at great length, and they felt confident that the Lady Vols could learn to execute it.

Summitt's defensive strategy has always been based on a strong "man" defense. Having players match up "eyeball to eyeball" is a trademark of Pat's coaching style. In fact, Summitt often uses the zone defense as a threat to motivate her team to play better player-to-player. More than once she has said in her halftime exhortations, "If you don't play better player-to-player defense, we're going to a 2-3 zone and let them beat us."

So it was ironic that at the end of the season, the Lady Vols found themselves practicing the dreaded zone. Having a Summitt-coached team use it for any length of time would indeed surprise the opposition. Having the Lady Vols execute it well would indeed surprise the Tennessee coaching staff.

Summitt was also concerned about the health of her players. "Bridge, no sprint work today," she said to Gordon, who was still recuperating from the flu. "You can make it up later." To Sheila, she said, "Stay away from anybody with a cough, sniffles, or heartburn. I know you catch anything that's going around. We've got to stay healthy for postseason."

After a Wednesday practice, the team left immediately by bus for Chapel Hill. They would spend the night in Tar Heel country, play the game on Thursday, then return to Knoxville late Thursday night. Since the University of North Carolina is about 6-1/2-hours from UTK, it would be another exhausting trip.

The game was an easy one. Tennessee won 88-65, a showing Sylvia Hatchell found respectable. "It could have been worse," she said.

With the North Carolina victory, Tennessee was undefeated in road games for the 1987-88 season. They also stretched their winning streak to 15. Since the final regular-season game was scheduled for Sunday in Knoxville against winless (0-24) Tennessee State, the Lady Vols were almost assured of tying the record of 16 straight victories set in 1977-78.

Records, however, were not the immediate concern of the Lady Vols. Rest was. They left Chapel Hill immediately following the game and slept as much as possible on the bus ride home. Their arrival time of 4:30 a.m. made it yet another very short night for those, like Kathy Spinks, who had 7:50 Friday morning classes. Nevertheless, the weary travelers were in high spirits as they crawled off the bus. The next game should be easy, and tournament time was only a week away.

Traditionally, the final home game of the season honors the senior members of the squad. As Dawn Marsh, Lisa Webb, and Kathy Spinks were introduced before the tip-off of the Tennessee State University game, the announcer read highlights of their Lady Vol careers, and Coach Summitt presented each one with a white carnation and a hug. The seniors were also featured along with Summitt on the program cover, and their achievements were detailed inside.

Another Tennessee tradition is that the seniors start this final home game. In keeping with that custom, Spinks replaced Frost and Webb replaced Tuggle in the starting lineup. Dawn Marsh, who had never lost her position to Kris Durham, was joined by McCray and Gordon for the opening tip. As if to prove she should have started more often, Spinks scored the first six points for the Lady Vols.

For the sixth time in the season, the Lady Vols soared over the century mark, and for the sixth time, it was Tonya Edwards who hit the 100th point. Despite the wide victory margin (104-51), the Lady Vols did not play particularly well, but with their 16th consecutive win, they tied a Lady Vol record. And they finished the regular season, which, it had seemed of late, was their objective. Finally, as Coach Summitt told them, "crunch time" was here. The conference tournament would begin in 5 days.

CHAPTER ELEVEN

Buddies

The first Southeastern Conference (SEC) women's basketball tournament was held in Knoxville in 1980, and until 1987 the championships rotated each year to the campus of one of the competing schools. In 1987 the decision was made to move the tournament to a neutral site, and Albany, Georgia, was chosen. Since that tournament was judged a success, athletic directors voted for the 1988 event to be held again in the south Georgia city.

The SEC has a long and rich football history, and in recent years men's basketball teams have done well nationally. Women's programs have fared even better. Women's SEC teams have won national championships in golf (Florida in 1985 and 1986), gymnastics (Georgia, 1987), track (LSU—indoor and outdoor in 1987, and Tennessee—outdoor in 1981), and of course basketball (Tennessee in 1987). Conference schools have also been strong in swimming, tennis, and volleyball.

In women's basketball, the SEC is generally considered the best conference in the country. This year, for example, Auburn was ranked Number 1 and Tennessee Number 3 nationally going into the tournament. Of the 10 schools that make up the SEC (Alabama, Auburn, Florida, Georgia, Kentucky, LSU, Ole Miss, Mississippi State, Tennessee, and Vanderbilt) only Florida and Mississippi State had not been ranked in the top 20 at some point during the season. The conference is so strong that people often claim one can see better basketball played at the SEC tournament than at the Final Four event.

By virtue of finishing the regular season in second place behind Auburn, Tennessee received a first-round bye and was not scheduled to play until Saturday, March 5, at 7:00 p.m. The Lady Vols' first game would be against the winner of the Friday night game between Vandy and Kentucky. Then, if the tournament went according to predictions and seeding, Tennessee and Auburn would play in the finals on Monday night, March 7. The tournament did in fact proceed according to plan, but to get there Tennessee had to defeat Kentucky and Georgia. Auburn, with a somewhat easier bracket befitting the Number 1 seed, defeated Mississippi State and Ole Miss before the confrontation with Tennessee.

In preparation for the tournament, sport psychologist Tina Buckles had the team select buddies. Players formed groups of three, so when they needed support they could talk with a buddy. As Tina pointed out, "Teams do this naturally, but by structuring it, perhaps every athlete will benefit, not just the ones with close friends."

Whitey Hitchcock also contributed a special pregame strategy. Ever-striving to increase the conditioning edge, he had reinstituted the 400-yard runs 4 weeks before the tournament. On Tuesday before Tennessee's opening game on Friday, the Lady Vols ran eight 400-yard sprints, and then were timed in a 200-yard run.

They finished the 200 yards in 32 to 33 seconds, which, Whitey noted, was extremely fast after all those long 400-yard sprints. But when Holly Warlick learned of the workout, she worried that the sprints may have been counterproductive, further exhausting her already exhausted players.

Indeed, Tennessee did seem lethargic in the first half of their game against Kentucky. But as in the regular-season game, the Lady Vols came on strong in the second period to win, 100-66. Dawn Marsh played extremely well, scoring 14 points and handing off seven assists. Bridgette Gordon, recovered from the flu, led Tennessee in scoring with 20.

For Kentucky, Jodie Whitaker again had a tremendous game, leading everybody in scoring with 28 points. For the first time, it was Kris Durham, not Tonya Edwards, who hit the 100-point mark, with a three-pointer. But Durham injured her little finger, and during Summitt's postgame rap, trainer Jenny Moshak packed Durham's hand in ice.

Tennessee's next opponent was Georgia. As a fan remarked, "When Coach Summitt's team meets Coach Landers's team, there is only one word to describe it—WAR." As with all wars, emotions run high. Coaches deliberately appear nonchalant and players mimic the coaches, but underneath the facades, everyone connected with both teams was consumed with thoughts of the upcoming game and with the desire to win.

Pat Head Summitt prepared her squad by telling them, on the morning before the game, exactly what she expected Georgia to do. First, she explained the strengths and weaknesses of each Georgia player. "Carla Green takes a lot of shots and is shooting 40 percent," she said. "She shoots more off penetration, but will not shoot outside." Regarding point guard Adrienne Shuler, Summitt said, "She's a fine player, only a freshman. Make her handle the ball with her left hand." About Jill Mitchell: "She played 20 minutes in yesterday's victory over LSU (86-84) and was one for four from the field. She was a little tentative, but forget that. She won't be tentative against us."

Next, Summitt explained the various Georgia offenses. "When they call 'motion' or show a fist, they are running the same offense out of a 1-2-2 set," she said. "They may set it high or low. Ole Miss and Texas run the same thing." Then Summitt and the other coaches demonstrated as the players walked through their defense against Georgia's "fist." The team also prepared itself for each of Georgia's other offensive patterns.

Afterward, the Lady Vols sat in a semicircle to discuss strategy. Summitt interspersed her explanations with questions directed to her team: "Got that, Bridge?" or "Melissa, can you handle that?" The players asked specific questions such as, "How come they got so many baskets off that curl play out-of-bounds when we played at Georgia?" Summitt explained ways to defend against problem situations. Players were also asked their opinions about different strategies, and Bridgette Gordon, as usual, had the most helpful comments. Kris Durham, still nursing a sore finger, was unusually quiet. X rays had revealed no broken bones in her finger and the team doctor, Pat Eachus, had cleared Durham to play, but because the hand was heavily bandaged, Summitt had decided the freshman point guard would sit out.

The Lady Vol preparation for the Georgia game is typical of the approach taken by most coaches, but few coaches exude the same confidence as Pat Summitt. Everybody at that Sunday morning session knew Tennessee would be victorious against Georgia that afternoon. Coach Summitt had willed it; it would be so.

From the opening tip, Bridgette Gordon was spectacular. The 6-foot junior made her first four shots and had 12 of UTK's first 24. Dawn Marsh, not to be outdone, established a UTK single-game and SEC tournament record with 18 assists, and had only one turnover. Uncharacteristically, the Lady Vols had their best performance of the season for the opening period and led at halftime by 11 points, 47-36.

Georgia did not fold, however. They pulled to within two points of the Lady Vols with 2 minutes left in the game. At that point, Melissa McCray scored on a 10-foot shot from the baseline, followed by a jumper at the free throw line to seal the victory for Tennessee. The final score was 82-76.

After the game Coach Summitt told her team, "You showed good mental toughness to hold on under pressure. I'm proud of you. You got us to the championship game, which is where we wanted to be." She concluded with "Congratulations; I love you."

Monday, the day of the championship game, Tennessee practiced from noon until 1:00 p.m. in the Civic Coliseum, site of the 8:00 p.m. contest. To begin the session, Coach Summitt said to her team, "Good job under pressure yesterday." Then she became more critical. "We had nine offensive rebounds and only one of those by a post player. Frost had 1, Tuggle—zero, Webb—zero, Spinks—zero. We won the game with our perimeter play. Bridgette and Tonya bailed you post people out." She finished fussing at her big players by saying, "If we have those stats tonight we deserve to get beat. Some games you may struggle with shooting. They just won't fall. But you should never struggle on defense or with rebounding—that's a matter of effort."

Then, to reduce her team's tension over the upcoming game with Number 1 ranked Auburn, Summitt spoke reassuringly. "This game tonight is not a 'must' game. There is life after the Southeastern Conference. Of course it would be nice to win in terms of bragging rights and pride, but by getting to the championship game, we should be one of the top four seeds for the first round of the nationals.'' Summitt added, ''Today, let's play to improve our game.''

Holly Warlick then described the Auburn offensive patterns, and again, the team walked through them. Then Pat explained the defense she wanted her team to use to counteract Auburn. ''Vickie Orr's a great, great center,'' she told Sheila. ''If you get caught out of position, she'll abuse you. Make Orr score over you. Don't lunge out of position. The keys are denial, recovery, contest, and box. Got that?'' Sheila, who had not played well in the two previous tournament games, nodded somberly.

Mickie DeMoss pointed out that they were weak outside shooters. Said the assistant coach, ''They hit with some consistency when they get within 15 feet; outside of that they are definitely streaky.''

The Lady Vols concluded the practice by running through some offensive patterns and shooting free throws. At one point, Kris Durham, who was playing with a splint on the little finger of her left hand, made a poor pass. Summitt snapped, ''Kris, you gotta put something on those passes. Won't have you being tentative.'' Eachus, the team physician, had again given her okay for the freshman point guard to play. Summitt wanted Durham to play, not only to give her experience, but also because the team needed the athletic ability of the talented rookie. But Pat warned, ''Kris, if you can't pass better than that, you'll sit again tonight.''

After practice, Sheila Frost called on one of her designated buddies, Dawn Marsh. The tallest player on the team confided in the shortest player on the team, sharing her dismay at her recent performances. Marsh reminded her friend not to dwell on the past, as the team had agreed at the beginning of the season. She also reminded Sheila of something she was beginning to forget—that she is a talented player. By the time they finished talking, Sheila felt ready for the championship game.

The Tennessee dressing room before the Southeastern Conference championship game on March 7, 1988, was more like a beauty salon than a locker room. The Lady Vols, as well as the coaches, were busy using a giant can of hair spray; someone was yelling, above the din of booming rock music, for eye shadow, and Coach Summitt was switching from dark to light pantyhose. She made the switch after somebody said her hose didn't match the orange and beige suit she was wearing. Mickie, with a gleam in her eyes, said, ''You know why Pat decided on dark stockings, don't you. She hasn't shaved her legs since we lost to Auburn on January 9.'' Not shaving during a winning streak was a superstition dating back to high school days, and Pat wasn't about to change now. The reason for the extra concern about looks was that the game was being televised by 13 cable stations.

Primping completed, the Lady Vols seated themselves in a semicircle in front of the chalkboard on which had been written, "Let's do it." This slogan is another Tennessee superstition dating back to 1980 when Lynn Collins, in her freshman year, began the tradition. Lisa Webb became the designated writer when Collins graduated; when Webb finished her career this year she would pass the chalk on to someone else.

Under "Let's Do It," graduate assistant Heidi Van Derveer had written the name of each Lady Vol player and her average number of rebounds this season. The Tennessee defenses were also listed along with the Auburn offenses.

Pat, tossing the chalk in her hand, began her pregame remarks by saying, "If we lose, it will be because of two things: boards and not taking care of the ball. Our challenge to you is that every kid get one more rebound than your average."

Pat, after briefly reviewing the Tennessee defense and the Auburn offenses, finished her pregame instructions with, "Let's get 10 steals. We'll start in our zero defense. Constant pressure. Jennifer on Stewart. Sheila on Orr. Play like you did against Georgia: relaxed, air of confidence. Great challenge. Great opportunity. Auburn has the pressure cause they're Number 1. Let's go!" The team rose as one, and ran from the locker room amid cheers and shouts of "Go Lady Vols. Go, Orange!"

The game began with Auburn's scoring from all over the court while Tennessee "tossed the ball back and forth," according to Coach Summitt. After almost 2-1/2 minutes, Auburn led, 8-0. The Lady Vols had committed three turnovers and hadn't taken a single shot. Auburn extended its lead to 31-23 before Bridgette Gordon made her presence felt. She hit from the corner, had several fast-break lay-ups, and scored with power moves inside. Then, with 8 seconds remaining in the half and the score 38-37 in favor of Tennessee, Summitt called a time-out. Summitt inserted her best long-range shooters, Jennifer Tuggle, Tonya Edwards, and Kris Durham, into the lineup with instructions for one of them to attempt the basket from three point land. But as the seconds ticked away, the ball fell into Bridgette Gordon's hands instead, and at the buzzer, the tall forward launched a three-pointer into the basket. On their way to the locker room, Summitt turned to her assistants and said wryly, "Wasn't that great coaching?"

The mood in the Lady Vol dressing room was subdued. Pat's main criticism was directed at Dawn Marsh. "Dawn, you're not taking charge on offense. Come on. We're making Auburn's zone look huge. Melissa, Bridgette, Dawn, attack!''

Summitt was pleased with her team's defense. Orr had hit only 5 of 17 from the field, and, due largely to pressure by the Lady Vols, the Lady Tigers had shot a dismal 37.5 percent. As halftime came to a close, Pat had one final comment: "Twenty minutes—you decide what this season means to you."

At the beginning of the second half, it appeared that the season meant a great deal to Tennessee. The women in orange were playing inspired basketball: Bridgette was hitting from everywhere, Tonya Edwards was scoring and rebounding well, and Sheila Frost was magnificent on defense. The 6-4 junior was intimidating the awesome 6-3 Orr.

But the Lady Tigers fought back to 64-59 when Gordon was called for her fourth foul with 5-1/2 minutes left in the game. With Gordon out of the Tennessee lineup, Auburn managed to pull within three points, but when Bridgette reentered the game with 3:06 remaining, she was immediately fouled and converted the two free throws.

Lisa Webb hit a clutch 12-footer, and Tonya Edwards made both ends of a one-and-one to give UTK a 71-65 lead with 36 seconds left. Tennessee fans breathed a sigh of relief. That sigh became a moan, however, when Auburn's Dianne McNeil hit a three-pointer. With 28 seconds remaining, Auburn trailed 71-68.

Gordon missed a free throw for UTK, and Sharon Stewart missed one for Auburn; then Frost coolly stepped to the line and made two free throws to preserve the Tennessee victory. With 4 seconds left, Orr made a meaningless bucket. Final score: Tennessee—73, Auburn—70.

With the victory, Tennessee not only avenged the January 9 loss to Auburn, but also became the Southeastern Conference women's basketball champions for the third time in its 9-year history.

As the buzzer sounded, Lady Vol Boost-Hers who had made the 8-hour trip to Albany swarmed onto the floor with hugs and cheers for the Tennessee team and coaches. Lisa Webb cut the net from the basket. Dawn, Bridgette, Tonya, and Sheila went to the press room for interviews while the rest of the Lady Vols continued to receive congratulations from well-wishers and to sign autographs for the many children in the crowd.

Shortly after the game, awards were presented. The entire Lady Vol team ran to center court to accept the championship plaque. The most valuable player, to the surprise of no one, was Bridgette Gordon. She was deservedly the unanimous choice based on her 86-point and 23-rebound performance in the three tournament games. Her Auburn statistics were spectacular: a career-high 34 points (13 of 18 from the field), six rebounds, four assists, two steals, and one blocked shot. Coach Summitt told the press, "Bridgette is the best forward in the women's game."

There was some grumbling from Ole Miss and Lady Vol partisans because none of their players, with the exception of MVP Gordon, made the All-Tournament team. The lack of Lady Vol representation, however, exemplified the strength of the team and the Summitt philosophy. All 10 Lady Vols made significant contributions to the team's success, with only one dominant star, and Tennessee had even managed to win when Gordon was sick or not playing well. A team that does not rely too heavily on one individual is a trademark of the Tennessee head coach.

When the award ceremony was over, the Lady Vols hurriedly showered and dressed. They then stopped by the hospitality room where they filled grocery bags with sandwiches, candy, and soft drinks. It would be a long bus ride to Knoxville and there would be no stopping for late-night snacks.

The team had flown commercially to Albany, but to make it back in time for classes, a bus was sent to bring them home. It would be an all-night ride, but at least they could attend those all-important classes on Tuesday, which was the last day of regular classes for the winter quarter. A week of exams would follow, but at least the Lady Vols would be in town during that time. It was almost midnight when the bus carrying the Southeastern Conference Women's Basketball Champions left the parking lot of the Civic Center in Albany, Georgia.

As the bus pulled away, Coach Summitt walked down the aisle and said, "I'm sorry I didn't get to speak to you in the dressing room after the game. There was just too much confusion, but I do want to say how proud I am of you. You were great." She went on to thank them individually, with special praise for the defensive performance of Sheila Frost. Sheila had had her best defensive game in her 3 years as a Lady Vol, Summitt said.

Pat next turned her attention to Mickie DeMoss and said, "Congratulations to Mickie on her first Southeastern Conference championship." Laughing, Summitt added, "How long you been in the league, Mick?" There was a thundering roar from the players, who knew of Mickie's history of coaching at Florida and Auburn. Then someone yelled, "Now Mickie along with the rest of us will get the prize—a championship ring."

Festivities over, Pat consulted with Jenny Moshak, the trainer, and then asked the team if they would mind being tested for drugs when they got back to Knoxville. Expected arrival time was around 6:00 a.m., and if they went straight to the training room, they could be tested then instead of having to get up early on another morning. The team agreed, and Moshak requested that the athletes not go to the bathroom after 1:00 a.m. If they did, the urine sample necessary for the test would be invalid. Dawn moaned, "And I just drank three cokes."

With Coach Summitt sitting directly behind the driver, coaching him to drive faster, the bus pulled into Stokely at exactly 5:30 a.m. As the team gathered themselves together, Mickie announced over the bus microphone, "Make those classes. You can crash after that! No practice today or tomorrow, see you Thursday at the regular time."

CHAPTER TWELVE

From Play Days to Million-Dollar Budgets

To understand how far women's sports in general, and the UTK program in particular, have come, and how fast, it is helpful to think back to 1972, when farsighted women's sports professionals were just beginning to dream of such things as national championships for women. That was the year Title IX, the federal legislation that prohibits sex discrimination in schools and colleges receiving federal funds, was passed. The legislation, part of the Educational Amendments of the 1964 Civil Rights Act, included specific guidelines for physical education and athletics and required full implementation by 1978. Since intercollegiate athletics for women was practically nonexistent on most college campuses and Title IX mandated equal opportunity, the legislation caused considerable distress for college administrators. In response to the legislation, committees were established to study women's athletics and to make recommendations regarding compliance.

UTK was typical of most large state universities. The chancellor, Jack Reese, appointed a Task Force on Intercollegiate Athletics for Women on May 13, 1975, and the recommendations of that group, which were accepted by the chancellor on April 1, 1976, are the basis for the current women's athletic program on the UTK campus. By contrast, small schools and women's colleges often provided intercollegiate athletic opportunities long before it was mandated by law.

To imagine the context out of which Title IX arose, consider the decades of the twenties, thirties, forties, and fifties, which can best be described as the Intramural Era in women's athletics. The traditional team sports of volleyball, basketball, and softball were usually offered, and individual sports such as badminton, golf, tennis, and swimming were interspersed with the team sports throughout the school year to provide a variety of activities. In most universities, intramurals were dominated by sororities, and it was not unusual for women to be rushed by sororities because of their athletic ability.

In addition, universities occasionally sponsored play days and sports days for women. For play days, individuals from several schools gathered at one school to participate in a multisport, "superstar"-type competition. For sports days, several schools brought teams of players to tournaments at a host school. At both play days and sports days, emphasis was on participation, socialization, play for play's sake, and other ideals of sportsmanship. The days always ended with refreshments so the students could socialize.

The demise of play days and sports days at UTK came about in 1959 when East Tennessee State University sponsored an invitational volleyball tournament. A trophy, of all things, was awarded to the winning team, which happened to be UTK. Despite the success of the tournament, which was held annually until 1975, it was discontinued because, in the words of the tournament's originator and director Connie Mynatt-Axamethy, "It became too professional."

This thinking was typical of the day. Women leaders of physical education organizations resisted competitive sport because of what they perceived to be its inherent evils, and because of the prevalent societal view that women were physiologically and psychologically unable to cope with the demands of intense competition. In addition, there was a subtle, often unspoken fear that women who participated in sports would become masculinized as a result of such competition.

In the early sixties, UTK had women's teams in basketball and volleyball, but the schedule consisted mostly of games with Carson-Newman, Maryville, and East Tennessee State. Carson-Newman, under the direction of Mae Iddins, sponsored a basketball tournament during these years that was well attended by schools in Tennessee.

One of those trips to Carson-Newman provides another indication of the thinking of the time. The UTK team had one black player, and for her to be allowed to play, Iddins had to get special permission from her superiors. The permission was granted for Carolyn Baxter, the player in question, to be allowed to play, but she was not permitted to attend the social function following the game. To avoid any embarrassment to Carolyn and to protest the decision, the Tennessee team played, but did not stay for the social.

Those teams in the sixties were composed primarily of physical education majors and were coached by members of the women's physical education department, who received no extra pay. Few records exist to document the play of those early teams. However, lack of documentation, financial support, and spectators does not mean that the participants during those early years derived any less meaning from their experiences than those who participate nowadays.

The growth of the women's program at UTK during the sixties was again a reflection of societal happenings. The rights of women in general, and the rights of women athletes in particular, were beginning to be discussed, and the seeds were being planted for the women's movement of the seventies.

In 1963, the First National Institute on Girls' Sports was held at the University of Oklahoma in Norman. The institute's purpose was to provide physical education teachers with information about organizing and administering sports programs for women and to improve teaching and coaching skills in the sports of track and field and gymnastics. Invitations to the institute were extended to three people from each state and the Commonwealth of Puerto Rico. The 200 who attended pledged to conduct at least one workshop when they returned home.

The 1963 institute, the first of several, was interesting for several reasons. The Division of Girls' and Women's Sports, one of the sponsoring groups, was an arm of the national professional physical education association (known in 1988 as the American Alliance for Health, Physical Education, Recreation, and Dance, or AAHPERD). This organization had resisted competitive athletics, arguing that they too often resulted in sports opportunities for the athletically gifted at the expense of the majority of students who needed physical activity the most.

The other sponsoring group, the Women's Board of the Olympic Development Committee, had nationalistic interests in mind. Stung by an article in *Sports Illustrated* in early 1963 concerning the poor showing of American women track athletes, the Olympic Committee felt compelled to begin efforts to correct the situation.

The sports institutes were among the forces that eventually led to the Association of Intercollegiate Athletics for Women (AIAW), the national sport governing body for women's sports, founded in 1971. AIAW was originally one of the divisions of AAHPERD, but in 1979 that relationship ended when AIAW established its own legal identity. The split became inevitable when AIAW approved athletic scholarships for women; the first of these were awarded in 1973. This signaled to the traditional physical educators that the student-centered, educational model upon which AIAW was founded was being superseded by the traditionally male model of business/entertainment.

In retrospect, the awarding of scholarships brought to a close the Intra-mural Era of women's athletics. Ironically, this decision by the AIAW delegate assembly caused many women who had spent their professional lives striving for women's sport opportunities to leave athletics and return to full-time physical education teaching. Sport programs were, for the most part, left to the more feminist element in AIAW, who were demanding total equality with men's athletics. Another irony is that this demand led eventually to the demise of AIAW and the takeover by the National Collegiate Athletic Association (NCAA).

In 1981-82, the NCAA sponsored championships for women at the Division I level, after having already sponsored them for Division II and Division III institutions. Schools had to choose whether to participate in NCAA- or AIAW-sponsored events. Most schools, as did Tennessee, chose the NCAA. The reason for this was primarily financial. The NCAA paid expenses for competing teams; the AIAW didn't. The NCAA was also considered more prestigious, and many of the athletes and younger women athletic directors and coaches preferred the male-dominated organization. Perhaps the most significant reason for the defection to the NCAA was that male athletic directors, in most instances, were in charge of choosing the institutional affiliation. With the demise of the AIAW, the last vestiges of the educational model of intercollegiate athletics became history.

The late Katherine Ley, president of AAHPERD in 1974-75, is credited with exerting considerable influence on the Title IX legislation. Ley, a fine athlete herself and an advocate of women's athletics, was nonetheless fearful that the majority of girls and women would suffer in terms of sport opportunities if competitive athletics for females were emphasized.

She spoke of those fears in an address at that 1963 institute at the University of Oklahoma. She began her speech by saying, "I am really proposing that we have our cake and eat it, too.'' She was referring to the idea that the United States could produce women national champions and at the same time provide quality athletic programs for females at all levels.

Ley continued her presentation by listing some benefits that champions enjoy, such as ''the satisfaction of achievement, the discipline and self-sacrifice necessary in the pursuit of excellence, the thrill of winning, and the disappointment of losing.'' She went on to say,

> There are many other benefits to be listed, but the point is that the little kid from Podunk Hollow who wins the 25-yard dash at the local fireman's picnic can derive many of the same benefits as the gold medal winner at the Olympics. There's a difference in degree and the amount of prestige, but that's practically the only difference. We must be concerned that every participant benefit from participation in sports because, as we become better individuals, we become a stronger nation. This approach does not deny the development of champions, but it does emphasize skill for many girls. Our great need is to raise the average performance by girls in all sports including gymnastics and track and field. I am not as concerned about our women champions as some people are, but if we had many, many more ''near-champions'' we'd be a better nation, and it is very likely we would have better national champions, too.

Katherine Ley and other educators believed that Title IX would result in a deemphasis of athletics at all levels since maintaining girls'/women's programs on a par with men's/boys' would not be financially feasible. By deemphasizing athletics, physical education programs would improve, and more students would ultimately benefit.

But Title IX did not result in any kind of athletic deemphasis. Ironically, contrary to the intentions of some of the originators, Title IX has provided the impetus for women's athletics to become to a great extent a replica of men's athletics. At the college level this has meant recruiting, scholarships, gate receipts, specialization of athletes, and scheduling of games and practices with little regard for academics. As is often the case with legislation, the full implications of Title IX are still being debated and decided in the courts. But just as the demise of AIAW marked the end of the age of innocence in women's athletics, it seems that with passage of Title IX, the last hope for maintaining a unique women's sport model was lost.

The passage of Title IX had an immediate impact on college campuses throughout the country. The situation at UTK was typical. For the first time, the university allocated $20,000 for intercollegiate sports for women. Faculty coaches were given one-half released time during the quarter in which they coached, and a coordinator of the new women's program was given one-fourth release time from her PE teaching responsibilities.

Although Title IX was passed in 1972, it did not become law until it was signed by President Ford on October 15, 1974. In the interim between passage by Congress and Presidential signature, hearings were held throughout the country. The National Collegiate Athletic Association led the unsuccessful fight to defeat the bill.

At UTK, Chancellor Reese accepted the recommendations of the Task Force on Intercollegiate Athletics for Women on April 1, 1976. The task force had spent a year compiling the recommendations, and the consensus that emerged from their numerous public hearings was that women's sports at Tennessee should be a mirror image of the men's. That consensus, however, did not emerge without debate.

Women coaches all over the country had for years argued over the direction women's athletics should take. As was true nationwide, about half of the women at UTK felt that women should have the exact opportunities as men. The other half fought for an educational model. These women feared that the revenue sports, which for women would probably be only basketball, would be emphasized and the nonrevenue sports would receive little support. The result would be fewer women participants at the intercollegiate level. This proved to be prophetic at UTK. According to the task force report, there were 120 participants in seven sports in 1976 with an additional 100 women trying out for teams. As of the summer of 1988, there are less than 100 women athletes involved in five sports.

Another primary concern of those favoring the educational model was that women athletes would be exploited. Like the men, they would receive athletic scholarships regardless of their academic capabilities, and would be subject to year-round practice and game schedules that would interfere with classes.

Those who believed women's sports should mirror men's argued that women deserved all the athletic benefits men had always enjoyed: funding, facilities, and qualified coaches. Without such opportunities, women could never reach excellence in athletics. Women espousing this view also felt that women would somehow avoid the corruption and exploitation common in men's sports. It was not in women's nature, they said, to be cut-throat competitors, to win at all costs.

These arguments raged all during Pat Head Summitt's first year at Tennessee. The discussions began in almost total obscurity in one of the oldest buildings on campus, Alumni Gym. This changed, however, in the spring of Pat's first year at Tennessee with the appointment of the task force on women's athletics. In the open hearings, most of the Alumni Gym arguments were voiced by general members of the university community. Women's athletics at UTK were no longer a secret.

In an interview published in the *Knoxville News-Sentinel* on December 5, 1974, the reporter mentioned that there were no athletic scholarships for women athletes at the university, and indicated that this was the way Coach Head wanted it. She was quoted as saying, "I wouldn't know what to do if we had scholarships. When I see 37 girls go out for basketball and work hard for 2 hours a day, I'm impressed. They are playing the game because they want to. I think all students who need financial assistance should get it, but playing for the love of the game is what it's all about."

By the next year, however, Pat was quoted in the *Nashville Tennessean* as saying, "There's got to be some kind of aid in order to compete. It would be impossible for three colleges to give scholarships, while three others in their area didn't." Pat's advocacy of athletic scholarships for women was supported by the task force, which recommended that 10 full women's athletic scholarships be awarded for the 1976-77 academic year. These were divided into partial scholarships: basketball, five; swimming, three; tennis, three; volleyball, three; and track and field, eight.

Among those first recipients was Holly Warlick, who was awarded a $600 track scholarship. When she switched to basketball, her scholarship came with her.

The task force was also concerned with the funding. Football provides the revenue for all male sports at UTK with the exception of basketball, and some members of the university community argued that women's athletics should also be funded by football. Athletics should pay for athletics. Whether the women's and men's departments should be merged into one is still being debated in 1988.

In the fall of 1976, the new women's athletic department at UTK was instituted. Gloria Ray, the newly appointed women's athletics director, moved into Stokely Athletics Center, and the first women to be awarded

athletic scholarships arrived on campus. Debby Jennings became the Director of Sports Information for Women, and Sue Carver became the first
women's trainer. At long last the university was taking seriously its obligation to provide women with intercollegiate sports opportunities.

In 1983, Gloria Ray resigned and was replaced by Joan Cronan. Cronan
now heads a department consisting of 15 full-time staff, 11 graduate assistants, and 3 secretaries. In addition, there is a multitude of volunteer student
assistants.

In 1988, five sports remain, but now all coaches are full-time and
only two are female (basketball and volleyball). None of the women's
coaching staff holds dual appointments in teaching. The physical education/
coaching arrangement ended in 1977 and has never been reinstated.

The number of coaches for each team has also been substantially increased, with at least two assistants hired to work with each head coach.
As was predicted, basketball is the only revenue-producing sport, and,
as such, merits more money and more coaches.

The $1.6 million allocated to women's athletics for 1987-88 exceeds
anything the task force envisioned during its 1976 deliberations. Yet
compared to the University of Texas, this is peanuts; they report a $2.8
million budget for their women's program.

Similarly, Pat Head Summitt's salary of $48,000 was unheard of for
a women's basketball coach in the seventies; Pat started at UTK with a
graduate assistantship worth less than $3,000. Today, Pat earns additional
income from speaking engagements, a contract with Converse, and summer
basketball camps, which brings her yearly salary to $70,000-$75,000.

The men's coach at UTK, however, makes a base salary of $68,000,
and also has supplemental income. His 1987 season ended with a 16-13
record; Pat's was 31-3. But Pat is not upset by the discrepancy. "If we
averaged 16,000 to 18,000 a game," she explains, "I would expect more
money, but Joan [Cronan, the women's athletic director] has made a sincere
effort to raise salaries, and I'm pleased with what she has done. I'm not
looking for handouts." Reviewing the phenomenal growth of women's
athletics in the past 15 years, one is tempted to resurrect the slogan (now
recognized as sexist): "We've come a long way, baby." Ironically, that
was the slogan printed on the back of T-shirts promoting UTK women's
athletics back in 1973, the year the university first allocated $20,000 to
the women's sports program. One can only wonder where another 15 years
of change might lead.

CHAPTER THIRTEEN

Crunch Time

Preparation for defense of the national championship resumed on Thursday, March 10, 1988. When players reported for practice that day, each Lady Vol handed Coach Summitt a slip of paper on which the trainer had written that player's weight. Pat took the paper and recorded the weight in a notebook. The head coach then informed the squad that they would practice on Friday and Saturday, be excused on Sunday and Monday, and resume postseason preparation on Tuesday. Following the 2-day vacation, the trainer would again weigh each Lady Vol, and the coach warned that they had better not have gained an ounce. "I thought our conditioning was a factor against Auburn and Georgia," she said. "We were in better shape than they were, and it helped us win; please don't abuse your bodies while on vacation."

With the team seated in a semicircle around her, Coach Summitt began her discussion of the Tennessee victory over Auburn. Said the coach, "I watched the film twice, and it's no telling what I would have done to this team if we'd lost. We won with great pressure defense and an exceptional performance from Bridgette.'' Pat paused and then continued, ''Dawn, you played well against Kentucky and Georgia, but only average against Auburn; Kris, Jennifer, and Melissa, you were below average.'' Pat then pointed out that had they lost at the conference level, they would still have received a bid to the NCAA tournament, but from here on out, one loss and the season is over. She said again, ''It's crunch time.''

Summitt then explained the format of the women's NCAA championship tournament: In the first two rounds, the games are played on the home court of one of the participating teams. At the conclusion of the second round, the remaining 16 teams (referred to in the media as the ''Sweet 16'') advance to regional play, with four teams being sent to various sections of the country. In 1988, the regional sites were as follows: Mideast—Athens, Georgia; East—Norfolk, Virginia; Midwest—Austin, Texas; and West—Long Beach, California. The four surviving regional teams would then travel to Tacoma, Washington, where the Final Four would meet on April 1 to 3 for the national championship. Tennessee, Texas, Auburn and Iowa were the top four seeds.

If it does its job well, the NCAA tournament committee seeds teams so that the top four teams make it to the Final Four, and the top two teams eventually play in the championship game. So despite being in the Mideast region, Tennessee would not necessarily be sent to Athens, Georgia. As it turned out, the Lady Vols were seeded Number 1 in the East Region. They would receive a bye in Round 1, play Wake Forest in Knoxville in Round 2, and, if successful, advance to Norfolk for regional play. Auburn was seeded first in the Mideast, Iowa first in the West, and Texas first in the Midwest.

On Sunday, March 13, both CBS and ESPN had special programs to analyze and discuss the 64 men's teams who received NCAA bids, and for days the tournament was the major topic on most sportscasts. The upcoming women's tournament, by contrast, was virtually ignored by both network and cable television.

As this is written, the cable sports station, ESPN, is conducting a poll to determine whether the viewing public would like to see more women's basketball on television. Another interesting poll would be to determine whether there are too many men's games on the tube!

Because the Tennessee women received a bye in the opening round of the NCAA tournament, their opponent would be the winner of a first round game between Villanova and Wake Forest. Mickie DeMoss and Heidi Van Derveer made the trip to Philadelphia to scout the teams. At the Lady Vol practice following their return, Pat asked Mickie to report on the performance of Wake Forest, who had beaten Villanova and won the right to meet the defending champions at the Thompson-Boling Arena in Knoxville.

DeMoss indicated that they were a smart defensive team with lots of hustle and several defensive alignments. Mickie referred often to the "gimmick" and "junk" defenses of Wake Forest's Demon Deacons. Parenthetically DeMoss said, "They're an all-white team."

Some wisecracker whispered audibly, "There must not be any black Baptists or Catholics." Notre Dame had been their other all-white opponent and Wake Forest is a Baptist school.

Ignoring the comment, Mickie continued her scouting report by saying, "They run about 30 different offenses, but our man-to-man ought to give them problems."

Following the scouting report, most of the practice was spent running Tennessee offensive patterns against the simulated multiple defenses of the Demon Deacons. It was a spirited workout. The Lady Vols appeared ready.

However, they did not play well against Wake Forest, particularly in the first half. In fact, with the exception of Lisa Webb, the Lady Vols were terrible, committing 14 turnovers. Pat Summitt said in her halftime remarks, "You've thrown the ball to the scorer's table, to the media, to everyone except each other."

To individual players, the head coach said, "Jennifer, you're letting your offense affect your defense. Don't worry or dwell on those shots not dropping. Forget it and play defense." To Tonya Edwards, "Tonya, you're playing like you don't have a brain—do you know what our five offense is?" Dawn was the target of most of Summitt's anger. "Dawn, that hook pass was just plain *stupid*," the head coach yelled. Pat then spoke to her senior point guard in a somewhat softer tone, "You've been reading and believing your press clippings." This was in reference to a feature article on Dawn's passing skills that had appeared the day before in a local paper.

After the team left the locker room, Pat asked Mickie, "Can they stay with us in the second half, Mick?" DeMoss replied, "Sure, in the Villanova game they were behind at the half by 11, but Wake came back to win." Wake was also trailing Tennessee at the half by 11 points, 40-29.

In the second half, the women from Wake Forest did indeed stay with the Lady Vols—for a while. But with about 12 minutes to play, Coach Summitt called time to make defensive adjustments and after that the game was never in doubt; Tennessee won 94-66.

After the game Pat said to Lisa Webb, "Lisa, that was by far the best game of your career. Congratulations." Lisa agreed with her coach as did the 7,628 fans. At long last, the 5-9 senior forward had played as well as she practiced. She scored a career-high 24 points in addition to a game-high 12 rebounds and an unbelievable four steals. In an interview after the game, Lisa was a perfect reflection of the Summitt philosophy when she said, "I'm most proud of those four steals."

Summitt told the team that she was concerned about the sluggish, sloppy play at the beginning of the game. "We can't afford to play like that in Norfolk. If we do, our season will be over." Coach Summitt then reminded the Lady Vols that their next opponent would be Thursday in the East regional semifinal game against James Madison University. They would practice in Knoxville on Monday at the regular time and on Tuesday morning at 11:30 a.m. before catching the plane for Norfolk. The coaches and players were anxious to return to the practice floor because the Wake Forest game had left the team apprehensive about their chances of repeating as national champions. They knew they would have to play much better at the regional level if they were to advance to the Final Four in Tacoma, Washington.

After James Madison University defeated Clemson in Harrisonburg, Virginia, to advance to Norfolk and the East regionals for their game against Tennessee, Shelia Moorman, head coach of the James Madison Dukes, held a postgame press conference. Heidi Van Derveer, who had been in Harrisonburg to scout the Lady Vols' next opponent, later told Summitt what Moorman had told the press. The Madison coach did not think Tennessee was as good as last year, and the defending national champions could certainly be beaten, she said.

At Monday's practice, Pat asked Heidi, "Do you think I should tell them what was said at that press conference?"

Before Heidi could respond, the entire Lady Vol squad yelled, "Tell us, tell us!"

So Pat told them, adding, "Moorman did say that Tennessee had some athletes, but the only one she mentioned was Bridgette." After reflecting on what she had told her team, Coach Summitt continued, "I agree with the Madison coach; we are not as good defensively as we were last year, but our offense is better. We won the national championship, though, with

Number 11 Kathy Spinks vs. Wake Forest

our defense.'' Pat finished with ''The James Madison view is one that is held nationally. Nobody thinks you're for real. You're not defending your championship but proving that you're good.''

The remainder of the Monday practice was spent working on defending against James Madison's strong post game. Summitt indicated that 6-0 Alisa Harris and 6-1 Sydney Beasley would be true tests for Tennessee's post players. Pat reinforced her concern about the strength of the Madison inside game with ''Sheila, you and Kathy have got to play well if we are to beat them and advance to the finals of the East regional.''

Before the game, the team gathered in the locker room for the traditional Lord's Prayer. This time, Coach Summitt announced that Melissa McCray would have a special prayer before the unison ''Our Father.'' Melissa's prayer was one of thanksgiving for the wonderful opportunity sports provided them and for the God-given talent of the Lady Vols.

The game itself was not much of a contest. The Madison inside game failed to materialize and Tennessee, as usual, played sluggishly in the first half. But the contest was not a showcase of women's basketball: The Lady Vols won easily 72-52.

Coach Summitt summed up her feelings about the game with ''You gave Virginia and Rutgers lots of confidence tonight.'' This was in reference to Tennessee's opponent in the finals: The winner of the Rutgers–Virginia confrontation, to follow immediately after the Tennessee–Madison battle, would face the Lady Vols at noon on Saturday.

Norfolk, Virginia, site of the East regionals, is famous for housing the world's largest naval base. It is not known for being a mecca of women's basketball. Yet Old Dominion University, located there, has won three national championships (1979, 1980, and 1985.)

For Lady Vol fans accustomed to an abundance of radio, television, and newspaper coverage in Knoxville of the Tennessee women's basketball team, the dearth of coverage in Norfolk was a shock. At the time of the women's regionals, the men's NCAA tournament was also in progress, and newspapers in Norfolk and the Hampton Roads area were full of results, human interest stories, and profiles. Local and national television were similarly inundated with the exploits of men's basketball teams.

Another shock for the Tennessee team was the Old Dominion Field House, where games for the women's East regional were played. The ODU facility resembles a high school gym in a poor school district. To say the least, it was a contrast to the comfortable, expansive, and aesthetically pleasing Thompson-Boling Arena.

According to NCAA officials, Old Dominion was the only school to bid for the East regional tournament, but the players wondered aloud why a nicer facility had not been been rented. The ODU Field House proves that topflight facilities are not necessary for winning sports programs; yet subjecting women's teams to such poor conditions is demeaning. Norfolk was not the only place this happened. The West regional was held in a tiny gymnasium at Long Beach State (capacity 2,200) where the temperature inside was over 100 degrees when Long Beach State defeated Iowa for the championship.

Drug testing is another demeaning fact of life in postseason play. At the conclusion of each NCAA tournament game, teams and coaches must return to locker rooms for a 10-minute cooling-off period, and then be available to the press for at least 15 minutes. The winning teams are then subjected to drug testing.

Not all members of the winning teams were tested; only the top six, as determined by number of minutes played. Following the James Madison game, six female couriers entered the Tennessee locker room and each one called the name of a Lady Vol. When Dawn Marsh was called, Marsh looked at the courier and said, "Oh, you're my pee partner."

The NCAA official smiled and replied, "Yes, we'll be going to a room next door, but before we do, will you please sign this?" Then the courier handed Dawn a clipboard with the regulations regarding the testing. Without reading it, Marsh signed the paper.

Though a relatively new phenomenon in women's athletics, drug testing is a simple fact of life for the Tennessee players, who are randomly tested throughout the year and also attend a program dealing with alcohol and drug abuse once each quarter. But Coach Summitt resented the timing of these NCAA drug tests. She wanted her team to scout the about-to-begin Rutgers–Virginia game, and the head coach knew that obtaining urine samples from athletes who have just finished a strenuous game sometimes takes hours. As Jenny Moshak, the trainer, pointed out, "Strenuous physical exertion causes the system to shut down."

Sure enough, Tonya Edwards and Bridgette Gordon saw none of the Rutgers-UVA game, and Dawn Marsh was there for only the last 8 minutes. Summitt was furious, especially after she waited another 30 minutes and Bridgette had still not appeared At this point, Summitt sent the rest of the team to the hotel while the coaches waited for Gordon to oblige the couriers. That finally happened at 11:30 p.m., 3-1/2 hours after the end of the Lady Vol game.

The Tennessee situation, however, was no more frustrating than what happened to the Virginia team, which defeated Rutgers in the second game of the evening. Their testing was not completed until 1:30 a.m. Fortunately, both teams would have the next day, Friday, to rest. Finals were scheduled for noon on Saturday.

Of course, the Lady Vols did not rest on Friday. They watched game films at 10:45 a.m, then went to the Old Dominion Field House at 12:30 for a 2-hour practice. At one point during the practice, Pat said, "Let's have the scrub team on the floor."

The scrub team generally consisted of the assistant coaches (Holly, Mickie, Shelley, and Heidi) and Jenny Moshak, the trainer. Today, though, Pat said to Jenny, "I'll play the post position, Jenny, you're not big enough."

The scrub team walked through offensive and defensive plays of the Lady Vols and their opponents as Coach Summitt explained the complicated maneuvers. Pat was uncharacteristically relaxed and jovial as she directed the scrubs and demonstrated post play. When Holly Warlick went in the wrong direction on one of the Lady Vol plays, Melissa McCray, seated on the floor and listening to the instructions, yelled, "Holly doesn't know our offense."

Summitt responded, "There goes your raise, Hol."

Several observers were at the practice. Cheryl Littlejohn, who had finished her basketball career at Tennessee the previous year, had driven down from Washington to see the tournament and visit with her former teammates. Littlejohn, who would soon begin training as a special agent in the Department of Justice, said the national championship had helped her secure the prestigious government position. Said Littlejohn, "Basketball opened a lot of doors. Two weeks after our return from Washington after winning the national championship [President Reagan invited the team for a White House visit], a lady called me about the justice department."

Kay Yow, Pat's assistant coach at the 1984 Olympics and head coach at the 1988 games, was another observer at the Lady Vol practice. Yow observed, "Pat's an excellent coach; I'm impressed that she continues to get better at what she does." Echoing what many others have said, Kay mentioned, "She's one of the most objective people I've ever dealt with— honest, forthright, lays her cards on the table—all wonderful attributes."

Practice over, the Lady Vols left for the hotel and a short rest before taking in an early movie. On the way to the Airport Hilton, the team stopped for a snack at Wendy's, then relaxed in their rooms before the movie treat. Some of the squad saw "Shoot to Kill" while others went to "Johnny

Be Good.'' After the movies, the Lady Vols and their coaches, along with Cheryl Littlejohn and Joetta Clark, a former Lady Vol track star who also came to Norfolk for the regionals, went to Steak and Ale for dinner. It was a relaxed affair, and the team ended the meal by sharing a huge gooey chocolate dessert.

On the way back to the hotel after dinner, Mickie said, "Lights out by 11:00. We'll be eating our pregame meal in the morning around 9:00, and we'll leave for the game at 10:50 a.m. You need to get some rest."

The finals of the East, West, Mideast, and Midwest regionals were all scheduled for Saturday, March 26. ESPN would cover all the games, beginning with the Tennessee-Virginia game at noon, and ending with the 10:00 p.m. game between Long Beach and Iowa. The Lady Vols would be able to fly back to Knoxville in time to see the 8:00 and 10:00 games.

Before the team left the hotel for their scheduled game against Virginia, sport psychologist Tina Buckles called Coach Summitt and said she would like to ride to the Old Dominion Field House in the van with Dawn Marsh. Tina wanted to help her relax on the way to the game. Pat concurred with Buckle's opinion and said, "We're leaving at 10:50; you can sit next to Dawn."

Upon arrival at the Field House, Pat went for a television interview and Mickie DeMoss went into the locker room to write the game plan on the chalkboard. Under Lisa Webb's "Let's do it," she noted the Virginia offenses: (1) fist, (2) Texas, (3) thumbs up, (4) 1, and (5) c. Beside each offense were diagrams of where the Virginia players would be positioned and cues for the Tennessee defense. DeMoss also wrote on the board the word *Keys* (to the game) and listed (1) take care of the ball, (2) make Virginia set a half court offense, and (3) attack on offense.

The Lady Vols, seated in their customary semicircle around the chalkboard, chatted among themselves while waiting for their head coach to finish her interview. It must have been 100 degrees in the antiquated dressing room. Lisa Webb, fidgeting in her chair said, "I'm about to monkey." Somebody asked, "What does that mean?" Jennifer Tuggle replied, "That's Lisa talk. What does it mean?"

Lisa explained, "My grandmother always said that when it was really hot." All the players agreed they were about to monkey.

Then the primping began when Dawn Marsh jumped from her seat, ran to the nearest mirror, and exclaimed, "Lord, look at my hair, and I'm fixin' to go on TV."

Soon Coach Summitt walked into the steamy room. "Every time I speak in public, I get butterflies. If I'm well prepared, they go away and

I do a good job. You're well prepared. You've got to have confidence that everybody can do it. Come on, step up to that microphone!'' The team ran from the room amid the usual cheers of "Let's go, Lady Vols!''

As they were leaving the locker room, Tina Buckles turned to Pat and said, "I think your relaxed attitude with the team has been great. Just don't let them get tight.''

Pat replied, "How does the team seem to you, especially Dawn?''

Tina responded, "Fine, relaxed.''

Relaxed they were. As they say in the trade, they put on a clinic for Virginia. Tennessee jumped to a 12-0 lead before the Lady Wahoos even realized what had happened.

But in the second half, Virginia came charging back from a 15-point halftime deficit to within 1 point (77-76) of the defending national champions with 1:09 left in the game. At this point, Dawn Marsh took charge. As Coach Summitt yelled "Penetrate,'' the senior point guard dribbled through the Virginia defense and made a spectacular underhand lay-up. She was fouled shortly after that and made both ends of the one-and-one. Bridgette Gordon added two more free throws in the final seconds, bringing her total to 20 and the final score to 84-76.

For Marsh's outstanding performance against both James Madison (10 points) and Virginia (14 points, five steals, only one turnover), the Lady Vol senior was named the most valuable player in the East regional. Joining her on the all-tournament team were Rutgers's Telicher Austin, Virginia guards Daphne Hawkins and Donna Holt; and her consistent teammate, Bridgette Gordon.

The champions of the East regional tournament returned to Knoxville on Saturday night. When they arrived, they were greeted at McGhee Tyson Airport by television crews from the three local stations as well as fans, family, and friends. It was, to put it mildly, a joyous occasion. Pat Head Summitt's team had done it again: Tennessee would be returning to the Final Four for the ninth time.

After hurriedly greeting the crowd, the players and coaches rushed from the airport to their respective homes to watch the television coverage of the remaining two women's regional basketball tournaments. En route, they had missed the Auburn and Georgia final, which Auburn had won in a hard-fought 68-65 victory.

Tennesseans were particularly concerned about the outcome of the Texas–La Tech confrontation since the winner would face the Lady Vols on Friday in Tacoma, Washington. Kris Durham said to the rest of the team as they left the airport, "Bring on Texas. We have a score to settle.''

But that did not happen: In a thrilling overtime game, La Tech defeated Texas 83-80, winning the right to face the defending national champions.

Long Beach State easily defeated Iowa 98-78 in the West regional, so they would face Auburn in the other semifinal game. The Auburn–Long Beach winner would play the winner of the Tennessee–La Tech contest to decide the 1988 women's Division I collegiate champions.

Coach Summitt and the Lady Vols began preparing for the Final Four tournament with a practice at the arena in Knoxville on Monday, March 28. They would also practice in Knoxville on Tuesday before departing later that afternoon for Tacoma. Pat wanted to get to the West Coast in plenty of time for her team to recover from jet lag. By leaving on Tuesday, the Lady Vols would have ample time to adjust to the 3-hour time difference before their Friday semifinal game.

At the Monday practice, Pat began by congratulating her team for winning in Norfolk. The next item on the practice agenda was the upcoming game against La Tech. Pat told the Lady Vols that she had called Van Chancellor, coach of the Ole Miss Rebels, whose team had lost to the Lady Techsters by 20 points in the semifinals of the Mideast regional. Chancellor had told her,''Pat, you're not going to like what I have to say. I thought your team was playing well, but La Tech is awesome."

Pat had responded, "Tech may be awesome, but after watching films of them for the past 6 hours, I feel I know them as well as I know us. We'll be ready."

Pat then handed the players a sheet of statistics from their regular-season game against La Tech. "Reflect on your performance in the first game," she said. "Look at your individual stats." The individual stats were not always great, but the final score of 76-74 brought back good memories: Sheila Frost had put them ahead by two on a last-second shot.

Next Pat said, "Now I want each of you to tell me two things I can count on your doing when we play them at the Final Four." When she got to Lisa Webb, the head coach remarked, "Lisa, you played 10 minutes against them in Knoxville and had zero rebounds." Webb responded, "I'm at a disadvantage to their inside people in both height and weight. I'll have to play smart offensively and defensively to make up for that disadvantage. I'm sure going to rebound the next time."

To Sheila Frost, Pat said, "Sheila, Venus Lacy abused you physically in the first game. You've got to be tougher in Washington." Then Pat asked, "Are you committed? There is a big difference between being satisfied in going to the Final Four and being committed to winning it all."

The team yelled in unison, "We're committed to winning it all!"

CHAPTER FOURTEEN

April Fool

The semifinal game between Tennessee and La Tech was scheduled for April 1, 1988, at 6:00 p.m. in the Tacoma Dome in Tacoma, Washington. Coach Summitt could not let the day pass without at least one ''funny.''

At 7:30 a.m. on the morning of the game, Pat called the hotel room of her two assistant coaches, Holly Warlick and Mickie DeMoss, and told Mickie that four Lady Vol players—Dawn, Sheila, Bridgette, and Tonya— had been hospitalized with food poisoning. Mickie was speechless. When she recovered, she asked Pat to hold on a second while she told Holly. Warlick was on the verge of tears. After allowing the full impact of the news to take effect, Summitt then said in a cheery voice, ''April Fool.''

Holly and Mickie vowed to get back at Pat. Fortunately, they had a great opportunity. Bettye Giles, the athletic director at Summitt's under-graduate school, had filmed in 1972 a game between the University of Tennessee at Martin and Lambuth College in which Pat had scored 20 points to lead UTM to victory. Unbeknownst to Pat, Bettye had the 16-millimeter film converted to a videotape and had sent a copy to Holly and Mickie. After Pat's 7:30 call, the two assistants decided that today would be an excellent time to showcase the basketball ability of Pat Head (as she was known in 1972) during her sophomore year at UTM.

Under the pretense of watching a highlight film, Mickie DeMoss announced to the Lady Vols that they should report immediately after shooting practice to Coach Summitt's room where the film would be shown. After everyone gathered on the floor around the TV set, Holly slipped the videocassette into the recorder. In a few seconds, a poor-quality black and white picture of a long-ago women's basketball game appeared on the screen.

Almost immediately someone yelled, "There's Pat!" Sure enough, there was 18 year-old Pat Head, ponytail and all, running up and down a dimly lit basketball court. Actually, as some of her players were quick to point out, Pat was not exactly running. Jennifer Tuggle's comment was typical, "Gosh, look at her loaf on defense." Another Lady Vol, equally critical, observed, "She's not even boxing-out on the boards." But when Pat would make a basket or an especially timely pass, everybody would yell, "Hey, look at that. Not bad" or "Great move, great shot."

As the film progressed, the players made other comments about such things as the small size of the players, the team uniforms, the lack of spectators, and the tiny gym, but most of the attention was focused on Pat. Summitt herself said virtually nothing. Mickie and Holly had their revenge.

And the players had their fun. They laughed and seemed completely relaxed. After the videotape, before the players left for their rooms, Mickie said, "Have a restful afternoon. Pizzas will be sent to your rooms around 2:00 p.m. We leave for the game at 4:45."

Leaving for the game at 4:45 proved to be almost a disaster. The bus driver had assured the coaches that departure time would get the team to the game in plenty of time for the 6:10 starting time, but apparently the driver had forgotten about traffic. The Tacoma Dome was 30 miles from the Hyatt Regency Hotel in Seattle, where the Lady Vols were staying. Negotiating that distance on a rainy Friday during rush-hour traffic was no small feat.

As the bus inched along at a bumper-to-bumper pace, everybody could feel the tension build. In an effort to help the players relax, Summitt said, "We've got plenty of time. Tip-off isn't until 6:10. We'll make it." They did make it, with about 30 minutes to spare, but the team had little time for pregame shooting before the ritual Lord's Prayer and player introductions.

Summitt rushed to cover the keys to the game, which had been written on a tiny chalkboard in the Lady Vol dressing room under Lisa Webb's "Let's do it." When she finished, the team ran from the room in great spirits amid the usual cries of "Let's go, Lady Vols! Let's go, y'all!"

Almost immediately, the mood shifted. La Tech won the opening tip, and passed the ball quickly inside to Venus Lacy, who scored over Sheila Frost as though Sheila were no more than 2 feet tall. That set the tone for the game. The first half was, as Pat later said, "embarrassing for the Lady Vols and their followers."

The score read 36-23 at intermission, and the Tennessee dressing room was not a place for the faint-of-heart. "I don't think I've ever seen Pat as mad," remarked Tina Buckles later.

"Oh, I've seen her that mad several times," said Lisa Webb.

But there was no disputing that the coach was angry, especially at Sheila. Intimidated by Lacy and Westbrooks, Sheila had not taken a single shot and grabbed only one rebound in the first 20 minutes.

Finally, after Coach Summitt had vented her anger and couldn't think of anything else to say to motivate her squad, she addressed the seniors. "Kathy, Dawn, Lisa, what can you say to get this team up? We have 20 minutes left."

Dawn spoke first. "We got to take it at 'em. They're not better than us."

Lisa added, "Come on, you all. We need you, Sheila."

Kathy Spinks said simply, "We're playing like we're scared."

Pat added, "If you don't pick it up, I'm going to sit down and not make any adjustments in the second half." She added, "There are some people who couldn't afford it who flew out here to support us. Come on, do it for them." Then in desperation, the exhausted head coach pleaded, "I've never asked you to play for me, but I'm asking you now—play for me. And if you can't play for me, then for God's sake don't give up." To hear Pat Summitt come close to swearing was a shock to everybody in the dressing room. The situation must be desperate. Everybody knew that, but none better than the players themselves who trudged wearily onto the court for the final 20 minutes.

In the second half, though, Tennessee cut the margin to five points. Would this be a repeat of the Knoxville game when Tennessee pulled off a miraculous victory at the buzzer? For a moment it seemed possible. But with his team leading by only five points, Barmore called time, made some adjustments, and in the next few minutes Tech outscored Tennessee 15-4.

On the sidelines: Pat and her Lady Vols

It became a matter of how badly Tennessee would lose. As it happened, the final margin was a respectable nine points (68-59) because Tonya Edwards hit a 3-pointer at the buzzer.

In the final tally, Tonya Edwards scored 16 points, followed by Bridgette Gordon's 15. Dawn Marsh, who failed to score in the first half, hit 13 points after halftime and played Teresa Weatherspoon, the spectacular La Tech point guard, on even terms. Kris Durham played with confidence, penetrated the Tech defense well, and was not timid about shooting.

Lisa Webb, Melissa McCray, and Jennifer Tuggle had, at best, mediocre performances, but the Lady Vol who was most unsuccessful was the tall and gentle Sheila Frost. In the entire game, she took only three shots and managed to score only 3 points, all on free throws. Her rebound total was six. Everybody was upset with Sheila, but nobody was more upset than Sheila herself. How unfortunate to have one of the worst performances of one's career on national television at the semifinals of the Final Four!

The Tennessee players were absolutely devastated. Everybody in the Lady Vol locker room was in tears, some crying uncontrollably. It was a long time before Coach Summitt appeared. When she did, the sobbing Sheila said, "I'm sorry I let everybody down. I don't know what was wrong, I just couldn't get into the game."

Melissa McCray replied, "Don't blame yourself, Sheila. We win as a team, we lose as a team."

Before the head coach began her postgame comments, she said to Kathy Spinks, who was almost hysterical, "Handle it, Kathy. If you can't, then get out of here." Kathy regained her composure almost immediately. Then the solemn, dejected coach sat down in front of the teary-eyed squad and began, "I want to commend you on handling the year the way you did. You were great under pressure." Pausing a moment, she continued, "But tonight I'm embarrassed because they played with more confidence and with more heart. We got ourselves in too big a hole in the first half and just couldn't recover." Obviously concerned about the effect the loss had on the seniors, Pat then said, "Lisa, Dawn, great career." To Kathy Spinks, "Kathy, Tennessee has been good for you and you've been good to Tennessee." Then to all three, "I'm sorry for all of you it had to end this way, but you can be proud of your time as a Lady Vol." More tears from the team. Then the head coach spoke again, "You've experienced more highs than 90 percent of the population; just remember that and learn from the lows. Without the lows, there would be no highs." After reflecting a moment, Pat said, "Maybe we were a little complacent. I'm sorry I let you down."

The head coach then asked if anyone else would like to speak. Mickie DeMoss, a picture of complete despair, said, "We should have worked on your emotional level. We let you down."

Melissa McCray rejected Mickie's assessment. "We were prepared for the game," she said. "I just hate it for the seniors."

Joan Cronan, UTK women's athletic director, who had entered the dressing room carrying the NCAA plaque for Final Four participation, was the last speaker. "Learn from this loss, but hold your head high. Be proud of the season and of yourselves. You always have been a credit to women's basketball and the University of Tennessee. We're all proud of you."

Louisiana Tech went on to defeat Auburn 56-54 in the title game to become the 1988 national champions. For the first time, a male head coach,

Leon Barmore, won the women's Division I crown. Second place also went to a male coach—Joe Ciampi of Auburn. The two female-coached Final Four teams—Summitt's Tennessee and Joan Bonvicini's Long Beach State—lost in the semifinals.

Most of the Lady Vol players did not stay in Tacoma over the weekend to see La Tech win the national championship. Only Bridgette, Tonya, and Sheila chose to stay for the finals on Sunday. Bridgette had no choice since she had been named a Kodak all-American, and was required to stay for an awards banquet. Edwards and Frost stayed to be with their families, who had made the trip to Washington. Coach Summitt also stayed in Seattle for the final game. Later, after returning to Knoxville, she would express how devastated she felt by the loss, how it would take several years to get over it. But for now she would make her escape after the finals, and spend a few days skiing.

The Lady Vols who flew back to Knoxville were obviously despondent as they boarded the plane in Seattle. But that mood lasted only as long as it took for all passengers to be seated and the airline attendants to begin their safety instructions. As the attendant stood in the aisle in the center of the cabin and began pointing as he informed the passengers of the various exits, Kris Durham and her sister, Karen, mimicked every gesture of the amused attendant. Before he finished, everyone who was aware of the mimicry of the Durham sisters, including the good-natured flight attendant, was in hysterics.

The antics of Karen and Kris were a great tonic for the depressed Lady Vols. Almost immediately, the entire Tennessee contingent seemed relieved and relaxed, as if a great burden had been lifted off them. The long season had finally come to an end and in spite of the loss, they would now have some time to enjoy being regular college students.

Nobody mentioned the loss for the entire 7-hour trip. Perhaps the hurt was too great, or perhaps it was because, as Shelley Sexton observed, "This is an angry loss. It is very hard to accept since we played so poorly. If we had played well and lost, it would still have hurt, but not like this." Or perhaps their minds were already on other things. They were all seasoned athletes, aware that a loss is, ultimately, just a loss. There was no self-pity, and throughout the long flight home, they exuded confidence and good humor.

The good humor was still evident when the team arrived in Knoxville about 1:00 a.m. Carla McGhee, still recovering from the automobile injuries she suffered in the fall, had also made the trip to Seattle. The first one off the plane, Carla rushed up the ramp to the terminal, stood just inside the doorway, and waved at an apparent welcoming crowd. When the rest of the team saw Carla waving and smiling, they began to primp and comb their hair in anticipation of the fans and the television crews. Melissa McCray, not far behind Carla, passed her still-waving teammate and was expecting glaring TV lights as she entered the waiting room. Imagine the surprise of Melissa and the rest of the Lady Vols when they realized there was not a single person there to greet the exhausted Tennessee women's basketball team.

"I'm gonna kill you, Carla!" screamed Melissa. The rest of the team thought this was an excellent idea, and they chased her through the terminal. Fortunately, by the time they reached the baggage area, several boyfriends had arrived to escort them home, and Carla's life was spared. The UTK campus police also arrived with two vans for those Lady Vols who needed transportation.

So the Tennessee women finished the season with a 31-3 record, the fewest losses in Lady Vol history. They had also set another school record with 22 straight victories. Cronan had said they should be proud of themselves. The sting of the loss seemed to be already wearing off, and perhaps they would soon feel that pride.

Meanwhile, no throngs had greeted them, as would have been the case if they'd repeated as national champions. As Linda Ronstadt sings, "Everybody loves a winner, but when you lose you lose alone." Unless, that is, you have teammates there to make you laugh at the flight attendant, to tease you about the waiting crowd, and to share a seat with you on the last ride home at the end of another long season.